CHRIST OUR REFUGE

Making it safely through the last days

NORMAN R. GULLEY

Pacific Press Publishing Association
Boise, Idaho
Oshawa, Ontario, Canada

Edited by Kenneth R. Wade
Cover design by Dennis Ferree
Cover illustration by Robert Hunt
Typeset in New Century Schoolbook 10/12

Unless otherwise noted, all Scripture quotations are taken from
the New International Version.

ISBN 0-8163-1324-5

96 97 98 99 00 • 5 4 3 2 1

Dedication

Dedicated to the workers in the
East Asia Association (Hong Kong)
and to God's saints in China.
I came into your midst and went away rejoicing.
You are a special inspiration in your commitment to Christ!

Contents

Introduction

Only four years to the next millennium! The year 2000 is just ahead. Planet Earth rushes toward its rendezvous with destiny. Final events are already underway, and soon the most stupendous challenge will break upon those who follow Christ. Confronted by a demanding Sunday law (Revelation 13:12) and a death decree (verse 15), not being able to buy or sell (verse 17), with the whole world against them (verses 3, 4, 12-16), believers will be thrust into a global crisis unparalleled in the history of humankind.

Yet this is the finest hour for those who love Christ. For us, there is an end-time mission, an end-time experience, an end-time privilege, and an end-time message.

Many look to the coming crisis and tremble. It is time to look to the coming Christ and be unafraid! Christ, not the crisis, is the focus. It is not *what* is coming but *who* is coming that makes the difference. Christ is coming. Soon He will vault through the heavens in the greatest rescue ever undertaken (Revelation 19:11-21). Before this, He comes through the Holy Spirit (John 14:15-18). He is about to pour out His latter-rain power (Joel 2:28, 29). He has promised, "Never will I leave you; never will I forsake you" (Hebrews 13:5), for "I will be with you always, to the very end of the age" (Matthew 28:20).

Christ, *not* the crisis—this is our focus. Christ *in* the crisis—this is our joy. Christ *through* the crisis—this is our victory!

Look up, fellow pilgrim. He is coming to be with us and take us through the final events of earth's history. He has never called us to come to Him and then left us. He asks us to abide in Him because He wants to abide with us. He says to those who fear coming events, "Come to me, all you who are weary and burdened, and I will give you rest" (Matthew 11:28). And when we respond, He goes on to the second invitation, "Remain in me, and I will remain in you" (John 15:4). For "if you abide in Me, and My words abide in you, ask whatever you wish, and it shall be done for you" (John 15:7, NASB). Imagine that—a blank check!

Paul was unafraid. Why? He said, "I am convinced that neither death nor life, neither angels nor demons, neither the present nor the future, nor any powers, neither height nor depth, nor anything else in all creation, will be able to separate us from the love of God that is in Christ Jesus our Lord" (Romans 8:38, 39). The preincarnate Christ stood with the Hebrew worthies in the fiery furnace (Daniel 3:25). The glorified Christ stands among the churches in the end time (Revelation 1:13, 20).

May the following pages bring you hope, for we are about to enter our finest hour *with* and *for* Christ. The time of the end is upon us. It is time to head home. In the coming events on planet Earth, Christ will be the ark to take us through the storm (Genesis 7). He will be the way through the final exodus (Exodus 14, 15), for "the Lord will be a *refuge* for his people" (Joel 3:16).

"The eternal God is your *refuge*, and underneath are the everlasting arms. He will drive out your enemy before you, saying, 'Destory him!' " (Deuteronomy 33:27).

Norman R. Gulley, Ph.D.
Professor of systematic theology
Southern College of Seventh-day Adventists

Chapter 1

Christe
Our Only Hope

"Three, two, one . . ." *Zoom!* Commander Howard E. Rutledge's F-8 crusader jet catapulted from the deck of attack carrier USS Bon Homme Richard. Another beautiful day, thought the executive officer of Fighter Squadron 191, as he sped across the Gulf of Tonkin toward Haiphong. He was all set for the job—two bombs, two air-to-air missiles, and four twenty-millimeter canons were ready to go. Coming through the clouds at six hundred mph, he sighted the target bridge northwest of Thanh Hoa.

Enemy shells were bursting all around him. From the tail came a loud *bang!* The plane shook but soon gained its equilibrium. Rutledge dropped his bombs and headed for the safety of the sea. Suddenly, there was a thundering explosion right beside him.

Instinctively, Rutledge pushed the ejection button and was thrown clear of the craft just moments before it exploded in a ball of flame. Shocked, stunned, but thankful—hanging there over North Vietnam—he blurted out, "Thank You, God!"—his first prayer in twenty years.

It was November 27, 1965. Looking down, Rutledge spotted a group of armed Vietnamese waiting for him. When he hit the ground, they captured him, dumped him in a truck, and took him to Hoa Loa prison in Hanoi. There he spent fifty-eight months in solitary confinement—that is 1,740 days! In terrible conditions, he braved the cold in loneliness. Many depressed

American POWs gave up all hope and died. As I interviewed Captain Rutledge in the Philippines, I learned how he survived when so many didn't. He focused on biblical promises, reciting them over and over again. Daily he recalled hymns he had once sung. Christ became his hope in that hopeless place.

Captured and freed

Daniel and John the Revelator had something in common with each other and with Captain Rutledge. Both Daniel and John were captured—a Babylonian captivity for the teenager Daniel (Daniel 1:1-6); an exile to Patmos for the aging John (Revelation 1:9). Both are types (representatives) of the end-time people who will be thrust into the ultimate captivity of the great time of trouble. "At that time Michael, the great prince who protects your people, will arise. There will be a time of distress such as has not happened from the beginning of nations until then. But at that time your people—everyone whose name is found written in the book—will be delivered" (Daniel 12:1).

John tells about Michael. "There was war in heaven. Michael and his angels fought against the dragon [Satan, see verse 9], and the dragon and his angels fought back. But he was not strong enough, and they lost their place in heaven" (Revelation 12:7, 8). Michael is a name given to Christ. It means "who is like God." It is a name given to Jesus when He stands up for His people. He stood up for the loyal angels in heaven and threw out the disloyal ones (Daniel 10:13, 21). He resurrected Moses against the protests of Satan (Jude 9), and He will deliver the end-time people from the greatest time of trouble (Daniel 12:1).

Revelation 12 gives an overview of the great controversy between Christ and Satan. It pictures this conflict in four major battles: the battle in heaven that led to Satan's expulsion (verses 4, 7, 8); Satan's struggle to destroy Christ during His earthly ministry, (verses 7, 8); Satan's attack on the church during the 1260 years (538–1798; verses 13-16); and the final premillennial onslaught during the end time (verse 17). The theme is Christ's victory over Satan in each of the three past battles, assuring victory in the final battle. Later, Revelation describes that victory (chapters 16-20). It is decisive, complete, and final. But there is an insight tucked away in Revelation 12 that has been overlooked by many people. The battle has been won already! Yes, already. Consider the evidence.

Immediately after stating that Satan was thrown out of heaven (verses 7, 8), Revelation pictures his arrival on earth: "The great dragon was hurled down—that ancient serpent called the devil or Satan, who leads the whole world astray. He was hurled to the earth, and his angels with him" (verse 9). The text goes on to explain that "the accuser of our brothers, who accuses them before our God day and night, has been hurled down" (verse 10). Clearly, the one thrown out of heaven is the one who has been deceiving and accusing people on the earth. This is not his ejection from heaven before Adam and Eve were created, but after he had deceived the human race, at the time of Christ (see verse 13). He was cast out at Calvary.

Verse 11 reveals the results of this casting out: "They overcame him by the blood of the Lamb and by the word of their testimony." Calvary was liberation day! Calvary was the determinative moment in the great controversy. Calvary was the decisive victory over Satan. All subsequent skirmishes, however deadly, must be seen in the light of that victory. There is no subsequent battle that can undo Calvary. Satan is like a loosing boxer who flings his fists after the final bell. He can still cause damage, but it does not count. Even though he still fights on, the truth is that Satan lost at the cross. Calvary is our hope. What Christ accomplished there for us means everything.

Importance of structure

Did you know that the books Daniel, Revelation, and The Great Controversy are all put together in the same way? Each is divided into two major sections: history and end-time events. Daniel 1 to 6 is mostly history for us; chapters 7 to 12 focus more on end-time events. Revelation 1 to 11 is mostly history; chapters 13 to 22 deal mostly with end-time events. The Great Controversy, chapters 1 to 33, are history; chapters 34 to 42 describe end-time events.

"Why this arrangement?" someone asks. Through the historical sections, God gives insights into what is to come. Ellen G. White put it well in her introduction to *The Great Controversy*. "It is not so much the object of this book to present new truths concerning the struggles of former times, as to bring out facts and principles which have a bearing on coming events."[1] There are facts and principles that will be repeated in the end time. I suggest to my students that they read the last chapters of The Great Controversy first, to become familiar with end-time events, and then go back to chapter 1 and begin reading the historical section, noting facts and principles in history that are like those they read in the end-time chapters.

You see, The Great Controversy begins with the destruction of Jerusalem in A.D. 70 and ends with the New Jerusalem after the millennium. It covers nearly three thousand years. It is really "A Tale Between Two Cities," the old and new Jerusalem. It tells of Christ's blessing, guidance, and presence during the Christian age and gives insight into what He will do for the end-time people during final events on planet Earth. It covers time since Calvary, with the victory of the cross decisively determining the ultimate outcome.

Daniel and Revelation follow the same pattern. The historical sections are like a sneak preview into final events. One goes to the historical chapters, and, as it were, pulls back the curtain to see what is coming. For example, in the historical section of Daniel, there are three death decrees (Daniel 2:13; 3:4-6; 6:7). Nebuchadnezzar issued the first two and Darius, the third. The last two are particularly instructive. "Bow or burn," said the first decree. Three Hebrews did not bow, yet when the king flung them into the fiery furnace, they lived! Those throwing the three into the flames were some of the strongest of Nebuchadnezzar's soldiers, yet they perished from the heat (Daniel 3:19-23). The lions' den decree had the same outcome. Daniel was thrown in and survived. Those responsible for throwing Daniel into the den were themselves thrown in and devoured (Daniel 6:21-24).

None of God's people died from the three death decrees. Only the enemies of God's people perished. This gives insight into the end time. The death decree of Revelation 13:15 will not affect God's people (although there may be some martyrs before probation's close [Revelation 20:4]). In the end, the death decree will result in the destruction of its perpetrators.

The focus of Revelation

The book of Revelation may well be the most misunderstood book in the Bible. Luther and Calvin, for example, rejected the book. Neither wrote a commentary on Revelation, although they did on other biblical books. Often Revelation is considered difficult to understand. Yet the book has a focus that is remarkably precise and profound. The book is divided into eight divisions (subdivisions within the two already mentioned).[2] Each new section begins with a throne-room scene (Revelation 1:11-20; 4:1–5:14; 8:2-6; 11:19; 15:1-8; 16:18–17:2; 19:1-10; 21:5-11). The focus is on Christ and the throne of the universe, where God is in control of the affairs of humankind.

The very first throne scene is a vision of Christ. He is pictured as standing in the midst of the seven churches (Revelation 1:13, 20), including Laodicea (Revelation 3:14-22). He stands near even the church that keeps Him standing knocking outside the door! The threat to spew Laodicea out of His mouth is real, but He longs to see even Laodicea repent. Laodicea believes she is rich and increased with goods and has need of nothing. Yet here is a church that depends upon itself, as if it is self-contained and has all that it requires to go through the final crisis. Christ stands among Laodicea to bring it to its senses. For without Him, Laodicea can do nothing (John 15:5). He stands at the door and knocks, hoping to gain entrance (Revelation 3:20). For without the abiding Christ, there is no passage through final events.

It is this Christ, standing among all seven churches, who is pictured with eyes of blazing fire (Revelation 1:14) and with a double-edged sword in His mouth (verse 16). These are remarkable details. Why? Turn to Revelation 19, where the second advent is portrayed (verses 14-21). In the coming advent, Christ is pictured with eyes of blazing fire (verse 12) and with a sharp sword coming out of His mouth (verse 15). What is the signifi-

cance? These two pictures of Christ, coming at the two ends of
the book, call the reader to focus on the Christ of the second
advent. Who is coming, more than what is coming, is of paramount importance. It is as if Christ said to John, "Before you
look at any of the events to come on planet Earth, take a long
gaze at Me, the coming Christ."

This is our greatest need. So many church members lack
assurance today. Many busy themselves trying to be good
enough, to be worthy for heaven. That is the problem of
Laodicea—preoccupation with herself. Revelation cries out,
"Worthy is the Lamb, who was slain" (5:12). Revelation says no
one else was found worthy (verse 4). Only the Crucified is a
worthy human (God-man). No one gets to heaven on the basis
of being good enough. There is only One who is good enough.
Jesus said, "No one comes to the Father except through me"
(John 14:6). So the first throne-room scene pictures Christ saying, "Do not be afraid. I am the First and the Last. I am the
Living One; I was dead, and behold I am alive for ever and
ever! And I hold the keys of death and Hades" (Revelation 1:17,
18).

When Christ had finished telling John about the seven
churches and about each one needing to overcome (2:7, 11, 17,
26; 3:5, 12, 21), then John said, "After this I looked, and there
before me was a door standing open in heaven. And the voice I
had first heard speaking to me like a trumpet [i.e., Christ; see
Revelation 1:10] said, "Come up here, and I will show you what
must take place after this" (Revelation 4:1). Before showing
any of the events to take place ("after this"), Christ invited John
to come up in vision and see what was taking place at the throne
room of heaven's sanctuary. This is Christ's prescription for
assurance. Look up and behold Him in control in the throne
room. Look long till that image is impressed deeply within your
mind, and then look at final events. Christ wants us to come to
study end-time events from the vantage view of heaven. I have
often thought that one day I would like to write a book on end
events from the perspective of our first day in heaven. That is,
to look back on end events from the vantage point of complet-
ing the passage through them.

What did John see? He saw twenty-four elders at the throne (Revelation 4:4). They were wearing crowns. The word in the Greek for these crowns is *stephanos*. A stephanos was a laurel wreath of victory worn by the winner of a game in the Olympics. A stephanos was different from a diadem crown worn by royalty by virtue of birth. When Christ promises the church at Sardis, "I will give you the crown of life" (Revelation 2:10), it is a stephanos. Some believe these twenty-four elders are redeemed humans, among those who came up from the graves after Christ's resurrection (Matthew 27:51-53; Ephesians 4:8). The number 24 is significant, because there were twenty-four orders of priests who ministered with the high priest (1 Chronicles 24:7-10; 25:9-31; compare Luke 1:5, 8, 9) in the earthly sanctuary.

So the first thing John saw was human beings at the throne with Christ. These humans had arrived. They were at the other side of end events. They lived beyond death. One day, end-time saints will be there too. It's just a matter of time. John's vision of human victors, wearing a stephanos at the throne, gives assurance to other humans still on the planet. But John saw more. The twenty-four elders worshiped Christ as Creator (Revelation 4:11) and as Saviour (Revelation 5:11, 12). They were focused on Christ in heaven because they were focused on Him in their human journey.

Revelation 4 and 5 reveal the inauguration of Christ after His ascension. "Who is worthy to break the seals and open the scroll?" Only Christ. The twenty-four elders sing a new song, " 'You are worthy to take the scroll and to open its seals, because you were slain, and with your blood you purchased men for God. . . . You have made them to be a kingdom and priests to serve our God, and they will reign on the earth' " (Revelation 5:9, 10). These words echo those found in the opening verses of the book: "To him who loves us and has freed us from our sins by his blood, and has made us to be a kingdom and priests to serve his God and Father" (Revelation 1:5, 6). Christ is being inaugurated as the High Priest, and joining Him are twenty-four priests to assist Him, just as in the Old Testament type. What does this mean? Christ wants human beings to witness firsthand the unfolding of salvation's plan, to see that every-thing is done fairly, and to be witnesses to His work for human-kind. That's the kind of trustworthy Saviour we have! Before speaking about any events on planet Earth, including end-time events, Revelation focuses on this Christ and His death for humankind (Revelation 4:1).

All will sing the new song

Most of the world is focusing on anything but Christ. Even many church members remain preoccupied with cares of life that crowd Christ out of their minds. So many drown their troubles through drink, MTV, videos, the fast life, or anything that will help them escape. But the escape does not bring peace or rest. It is fleeting and without depth. With this in mind, there is a remarkable insight in Revelation 5. The new song is sung by three groups. The four living creatures and the twenty-four elders sing it first (verses 8-10). The multitudes of angels then sing the song (verses 11, 12). "Then I heard every crea-ture in heaven and on earth and under the earth and on the sea, and all that is in them, singing: 'To him who sits on the throne and to the Lamb be praise and honor and glory and power, for ever and ever!'" (verse 13).

Here is pictured all humankind, saved and lost, at the close of the millennium, looking to Jesus and singing praise to the Lamb, to the crucified One. Across the heavens, in full color, a gigantic three-dimensional documentary replays Christ's sac-rifice for humankind. "Before the swaying multitude are re-vealed the final scenes—the patient Sufferer treading the path to Calvary; the Prince of heaven hanging upon the cross."[3] Here everyone will behold Christ on the cross and sing a response, but for many, it will be too late. What a tragedy that some will wait too long to sing God's praise. It reminds us of Noah's car-penters. They were in the ark when it didn't matter, and out of it when it did. Now is the time to look to Christ, behold the Lamb, and be saved. Be saved from fear of final events, be lib-erated from self and things, be free to worship and praise the only One who is worthy. For He alone is our hope.

Captain Rutledge survived his crisis in China. He fixed his

mind on Christ through reciting the Bible and singing songs from the hymnbook every day. An excellent way to prepare for the end-time crisis is to memorize Scripture and the hymns of faith. It would be well to spend a thoughtful hour each day, meditating on the life of Christ, particularly the last scenes.[4] He died the death that was ours so that we may have the life that is His. He plunged into the abyss carrying our guilt so that we can go free. He cried out, "My God, my God, why have you forsaken me" (Matthew 27:46) so He could promise, "Never will I leave you, never will I forsake you" (Hebrews 13:5). Behold this Christ, and be ready for the crisis.

---

1. Ellen G. White, *The Great Controversy*, xii.
2. I have gained insights from several sources relative to the structure of Revelation from the writing of Kenneth Strand, Mervyn Maxwell, and the two volumes on Revelation produced by the Biblical Research Institute of the General Conference.
3. Ellen G. White, *The Great Controversy*, 667.
4. See Ellen G. White, *Last Day Events*, 64.

Chapter 2

Christ
Our Only Saviour

Father and son gaze lazily at the white water. The railway drawbridge stands open; a large riverboat steams silently through. The sun blazes from a cloudless sky. Suddenly, it dawns on Dad. "It's only two minutes till the train comes!" he exclaims. He dashes to the tower to lower the bridge. He looks below to the gears and gasps. His son has fallen into them. There's no time for rescue. *Help! What can I do? This is my son!* His mind races. If the bridge remains open, hundreds of commuters will plunge to their death. If he lowers the bridge, his son will be crushed to death. Agony rips at his heart. He covers his face, pulls the lever, and lowers the bridge, just before the train thunders across. He looks at the people drinking coffee, reading newspapers, carefree. He bangs on the window and cries out, "My son died for you!" "My son died for you, and you don't know it!"

The Father's heart in heaven is torn as He sees a world rushing to perdition. "My Son died for you, and you do not know or care."

Why did Christ die?

In recent years, Seventh-day Adventists have suggested two possible answers to this question. One group uses the Substitutionary Model (SM) to explain the death of Christ. They hold that Calvary was a substitutionary sacrifice to pay human debt and satisfy God's broken law.

The second group uses the Great Controversy Trust-

18

Healing Model (GCTHM) to answer the question. They view Calvary in the larger setting of the great controversy, with Christ's death answering three basic questions—(a) does sin bring death? (b) is it death at the hand of our gracious God? and (c) is it important to understand that God does not kill any of His erring children?

Is one group right and the other wrong? Or is there room for aspects of both? Is one model really more confined than the other, or are both informed by the great-controversy worldview? In other words, is it correct to say that one model has a larger view than the other?

Thesis

We must submit our models to the judgment of Scripture rather than judging Scripture by our model. That is to say, the model must not judge Scripture and inspired writings, selectively using them and interpreting them from any preconceived ideas about Calvary and the great-controversy issue. Although God has invited us to use our reason (Isaiah 1:18), reason must not be the final court of appeal. Human reason must bow before divine revelation, or we are simply left with rationalism. It should be kept in mind that "those who are exalted in their own opinions will despise the blood of the Atoning Sacrifice, and will do despite to the Spirit of grace."[1]

The thesis before us involves the following major premises:

1. Divine revelation gives insight into the eternal dimensions of salvation's plan. These are staggering, and they dismiss any simple model of the cross.

2. Calvary is more than a demonstration to prove that sin brings death. Such is a confined view for the following reasons: (a) The great-controversy issues are far larger than "is God or Satan right relative to the wages of sin being death?" The question of death is a *subsequent issue after the controversy was launched.* (b) *The prior and larger issues of the great controversy have to do with the supremacy of Christ and God's eternal law.* Ellen G. White is very clear on this.[2]

3. In this chapter, I define "the larger view or setting of the

cross" as the full revelation of Scripture and the writings of Ellen G. White, rather than only a view of the great controversy representing less than all that is revealed. Properly understood, the great controversy involves aspects found in both models (and other models besides), and one must be true to all divine revelation to arrive at the larger view of Calvary.

The eternal dimension

There are past and future eternal dimensions to salvation's plan that stagger the mind. Concerning the past eternity, Ellen White says, "The salvation of the human race has ever been the object of the councils of heaven. . . . It has existed from all eternity. . . . So surely as there never was a time when God was not, so surely there never was a moment when it was not the delight of the eternal mind to manifest His grace to humanity."[3] Concerning the future eternity, she says, "It will take all eternity to comprehend the science of redemption, to understand something of what it means that the Son of the infinite God gave his life for the life of the world."[4] So Calvary comes with an eternity behind it and an eternity before it!

No wonder Ellen White describes salvation's plan as "immeasurable,"[5] that it "far exceeds the comprehension of the human mind,"[6] that it "is too high to be fully reached by human thought,"[7] and "increases in greatness as we contemplate it.[8] Do we realize what this means? It means that the more we study it, the more opens up to be studied. It is not a case of mastery. Rather, with the passing of eternity, the magnitude of the content of Calvary will be ever unfolding without end! "It cost an infinite price to deliver the captives of Satan from the captivity of sin."[9] Calvary is an infinite subject that will take an infinite eternity to understand!

Look what Ellen White says about the love of God: "All the paternal love which has come down from generation to generation through the channel of human hearts, all the springs of tenderness which have opened in the souls of men, are but as a tiny rill to the boundless ocean, when compared with the infinite, exhaustless love of God. Tongue cannot utter it; pen can not portray it. . . . Eternity itself can never fully reveal it."[10] No wonder, even as an inspired prophet, she said, "I mourn that my expression falls so far short of the glory of the truth as it is in Jesus."[11] What about our expressions by comparison?

Concerning the angels, Ellen White says, "They saw the Redeemer take step after step down the path of humiliation. They saw him rejected, denied, insulted, abused, and crucified, and yet it was something beyond all finite intelligence to comprehend the full mystery of redemption."[12] So even angels who gathered around the cross and watched Jesus die, even they could not comprehend the full mystery involved, and they were sinless beings of a higher order than humankind (Hebrews 2:7)! How much less can we sinful mortals comprehend, and we were not there to observe Calvary! In fact, Ellen White says that "the redeemed throng will range from world to world, and much of their time will be employed in searching out the mysteries of redemption. And throughout the whole stretch of eternity, this subject will be continually opening to their minds."[13]

No wonder there are so many atonement theories! It is a humbling fact that the sum total of all the theories fails to do justice to what is known of Calvary now, let alone the eternal revelation of Calvary yet to come. This chapter included! At best, it is only a small glimmer, a grasping at the outer edges, a tiny beginning. I want to make it clear that many honest, conscientious people have given much thought to this mystery. The fact is, no one has arrived yet, nor will they ever! How humbly we should go to divine revelation seeking for more insights, rather than going to it with a tidy model seeking further corroboration. It is good that we communicate our understanding with each other. But in this exchange, all human thinking must be brought under the judgment of God's Word. For it is only in divine revelation that we have trustworthy evidence. Without divine revelation, we would not even know about Calvary.

Twelve Major Components of the Larger View of Calvary

1. The larger view does not confine itself to our gracious heavenly Father but also sees the centrality of Christ in the great controversy.

Christ indicated how the Old Testament spoke of Him (Luke 24:25, 26; John 5:39). The last biblical book is a revelation of Christ (Revelation 1:1) in the setting of the great controversy. In Revelation, the Father sits on the throne in the background (e.g., Revelation 5:6; 14:1-5, 14-20; 19:11-16). The war in heaven is between Michael (Christ) and Satan (Revelation 12:7-10), and Christ does not hand over the kingdom to the Father until after the destruction of "all his enemies" at the end (1 Corinthians 15:22-28). Scripture is much more Christ-centered than Father-centered.

2. The larger view involves all the Trinity and not just the Father.

All the Trinity suffered at Calvary. "God Himself was crucified with Christ; for Christ was one with the Father."[14] In fact, the Trinity has suffered from sin's inception.[15]

3. The larger view involves the eternal mediation of Christ and includes His priestly ministration in the heavenly sanctuary.

The larger view of Calvary believes "the intercession of Christ in man's behalf in the sanctuary above is as essential to the plan of salvation as was His death upon the cross."[16]

4. The larger view includes operation of all the divine attributes and not just that of love.

"Righteousness and justice are the foundation" of God's throne, says the psalmist (Psalm 89:14). As Ellen G. White noted, "When Adam fell, God's attributes of holiness, justice and truth could not be changed."[17] Calvary demonstrates God's justice (Romans 3:25, 26). Yet, by some, "love is dwelt upon as the chief attribute of God. . . . God's justice, His denunciations of sin, the requirement of His holy law, are all kept out of sight."[18]

5. The larger view must include Satan's attack against God's law.

This single focus on God's love, by Satan, opens up another dimension of the larger view of the great-controversy issues. "Satan declared that mercy destroyed justice, that the death of Christ abrogated the Father's law. Had it been possible for the law to be changed or abrogated, then Christ need not have died. But to abrogate the law would be to immortalize transgression, and place the world under Satan's control. It was because the law was changeless, because man could be saved only through obedience to its precepts, that Jesus was lifted up on the cross. Yet the very means by which Christ established the law Satan represented as destroying it. Here will come the last conflict of the great controversy between Christ and Satan."[19]

Christ "died to vindicate the claims of the law, to give to the world and to angels an unanswerable argument of the immutability of the law of Jehovah."[20] He even died "to provide a way whereby he [man] might keep the whole law."[21] It is therefore not correct to claim, as does the GCTHM, that law-giving at Sinai was only an "emergency measure."

6. The larger view recognizes the seriousness of sin and humans' need of salvation, as well as their need to trust. Humans need a Substitute.

The GCTHM is silent on human guilt needing atonement. It is a limited view of the atonement that overlooks the seriousness of sin as lawlessness (1 John 3:4), and more than just a disease that needs healing. Substitution is a major theme that runs throughout the Bible. Humans do not merely need healing; they need Christ as their Substitute (Isaiah 53:1-12; Luke 22:37; Romans 4:25; 1 Corinthians 15:1-3; 1 Timothy 2:6; 1 Peter 2:24; 3:18; 1 John 4:10).

7. The larger view is cosmic in scope, contributing to the understanding of unfallen beings as well as of humans.[22] Whereas humankind, unlike angels, needs redemption,[23] humankind, along with unfallen beings, needs revelation. To both classes, Calvary is God's response to Satan's questioning of His word.

8. The larger view of Calvary is more than a revela-

tion of God. **It is also an unmasking of Satan and an exposure of humanity.**

Because God is holy and true to Himself, He did something about sin and Satan at the cross (John 12:31; 14:30; 16:11). The cross reveals the unholiness of Satan and human beings, that as sinners, these created beings took the life of their Creator at the cross. John Stott addresses some of what we say here in stating, "All inadequate doctrines of the atonement are due to inadequate doctrines of God and man."[24]

9. The larger view of the cross must include all that Scripture says about Jesus. He is more than a Friend.

Christ is more than a Friend (John 15:15). He is our God (John 1:1, 14), our Creator (Hebrews 1:1-3), our Lord (1 Corinthians 11:26), our Master (Colossians 4:1), our Teacher (John 13:13), our Mediator (1 Timothy 2:5), our Saviour (Revelation 5:9-12), our High Priest (Hebrews 4:14-16), our Advocate (1 John 2:1), our Judge (John 5:22), and our King (Revelation 19:16). Calvary does demonstrate His love for us (John 12:32). It does reveal that He is our Friend. But, properly understood, Calvary shows Him doing for us that which we could never do for ourselves (Romans 5:8; Ephesians 2:8, 9).

The GCTHM proposes that we are God's friends, not His servants. Yet the larger view of the cross also includes Christ as the "suffering Servant" (e.g., Isaiah 42 and 53) and our response as "Christ's servants" (1 Corinthians 7:22; compare Romans 1:1; Ephesians 6:6; Luke 17:10; Hebrews 3:5; James 1:1; 1 Peter 2:16; Jude 1; Revelation 1:1). It is servants who will be ready for Christ's return (Matthew 24:45, 46) and receive Christ's commendation "Well done" (Luke 19:17).

10. The larger view is not a disclosure that demands priority over the claims of Scripture.

Any interpretation of the disclosure of Calvary must of necessity be in harmony with the rest of biblical revelation (e.g., "The Lord has laid on him the iniquity of us all" [Isaiah 53:6], or substitution). The disclosure at Calvary must not be placed above, or in place of, revelation in Scripture. Satan's disclosure in Eden, with alleged evidence concerning not dying by eating the forbidden fruit, was given to discredit God's Word (Genesis 3:1-6).

11. The larger view must include all that Scripture says about the cross. This includes all the biblical metaphors describing salvation.

It follows that the larger view of Calvary must include all that Scripture says about the cross, and not just revelation or disclosure. A selective use of Scripture is no different from Satan's questioning of God's Word relative to whether death will come through sin (Genesis 3:1-6), because in both instances, the reason of a created being is placed above a "thus saith the Lord." Authentic trust in God includes trusting in all of Scripture. Authentic trust in God is demonstrated by trusting in the totality of divine revelation.

12. The larger view includes redemption as well as revelation, and redemption necessarily has priority over revelation as its content.

Relative to human salvation, the larger view of Calvary, as given throughout Scripture, involves redemption (e.g., Matthew 20:28; Romans 3:24; 5:9) as well as revelation (John 12:32; Romans 2:4). Redemption is the objective side of atonement, and revelation is the subjective side. The objective side necessarily has priority over the subjective; otherwise, the revelation would be without meaningful content.

Redemption includes justice as well as mercy

Redemption includes justice as well as mercy (love). God is "a righteous God and a Savior" (Isaiah 45:21; compare Zephaniah 3:5). Of Christ it is prophesied He is "righteous and having salvation" (Zechariah 9:9). Jesus said, "My judgment is just" (John 5:30). Peter, in speaking to the Jews about Jesus, said, "You disowned the Holy and Righteous One" (Acts 3:14). And Stephen spoke of Jesus as "the Righteous One" (Acts 7:52). Scripture reveals God—and Jesus—in more than the one attribute of love. He is also righteous and just. Given that God does what He does because He is who He is, then the sum total of His attributes is in all that He does, including Calvary. That means Calvary must be more than a revelation of love. It must also be a revelation of righteousness, a revelation of justice, a revelation of the sum total of God's attributes. Having said that, we will confine ourselves to justice and mercy.

Ellen G. White speaks of the larger view of the atonement in the context of the great controversy. She says, "God's love has been expressed in His justice no less than in His mercy. Justice is the foundation of His throne, and the fruit of His love. It had been Satan's purpose to divorce mercy from truth and justice. . . .

"By His life and His death, Christ proved that God's justice did not destroy His mercy, but that sin could be forgiven, and that the law is righteous, and can be perfectly obeyed. Satan's charges were refuted. God had given man unmistakable evidence of His love.

"Another deception was now to be brought forward. Satan declared that mercy destroyed justice, that the death of Christ abrogated the Father's law. Had it been possible for the law to be changed or abrogated, then Christ need not have died. But to abrogate the law would be to immortalize transgression, and place the world under Satan's control. It was because the law was changeless, because man could be saved only through obedience to its precepts, that Jesus was lifted up on the cross. Yet the very means by which Christ established the law Satan represented as destroying it. Here will come the last conflict of the great-controversy between Christ and Satan."[25]

Here we see that any great-controversy view of Calvary must discuss Satan's attempt to divide God's attributes, focusing on justice more than mercy before the cross and upon mercy more than justice after the cross.

Redemption Includes God's Wrath

God's wrath is as far distanced from human wrath as is His love or any other attribute. Any attribute of God, such as wrath, must be considered as compatible with His attribute of love. God's attributes are no more mutually exclusive than are the three Members of the Trinity. These apparently opposite attributes (from a human perspective) belong naturally together within each member of the Godhead, as does each member.

The second advent is portrayed as "the day of God's wrath" (Romans 2:5), "for the great day of their wrath has come, and who can stand?" (Revelation 6:17). The twenty-four elders, at God's throne, have no question about God's wrath. With the second advent in mind, they know that the time of God's "wrath has come" (Revelation 11:16-18), for to Babylon God gives a "cup filled with the wine of the fury of his wrath" (Revelation 16:19). The eschatological reaping is likened to grapes cast "into the great winepress of God's wrath" (Revelation 14:19). The seven last plagues are "filled with the wrath of God" (Revelation 15:7), and with them God's wrath is poured out on the earth (Revelation 16:1), and with them "God's wrath is completed" (Revelation 15:1).

The remrkable fact is that Jesus, the One who said, "Anyone who has seen me has seen the Father" (John 14:9), is inextricably identified with eschatological wrath. The apostle John, who records Christ's affirmation of Himself as the revelation of the Father (in John 14), also pictures Christ as coming to war in the second advent phase of Armageddon (in Revelation 19). "With justice he judges and makes war" (Revelation 19:11). "Out of his mouth comes a sharp sword with which to strike down the nations.'He will rule them with an iron scepter.' He treads the winepress of the fury of the wrath of God Almighty. On his robe and on his thigh he has this name written: KING OF KINGS AND LORD OF LORDS" (Revelation 19:15, 16). The psalmist says, "At the time of your appearing you will make them like a fiery furnace. In his wrath the Lord will swallow them up, and his fire will consume them" (Psalm 21:9). "He will crush kings on the day of his wrath" (Psalm 110:5). Isaiah concurs, saying it is a day "with wrath and fierce anger" (Isaiah 13:9), in which "the heavens tremble; and the earth will shake from its place at the wrath of the Lord Almighty, in the day of his burning anger" (Isaiah 13:13). Zephaniah adds, "In the fire of his jealousy the whole world will be consumed" (Zephaniah 1:18). John says multitudes will cry out to be hidden "from the wrath of the Lamb!" (Revelation 6:16).

How balanced Scripture is! How unlike the natural world to associate a lamb with wrath. Yet in the God of "holy love," lamblike and wrathful qualities exist side by side without contradiction. This is why Jesus, the "Lamb of God" (John 1:29), is also "the Lion of the tribe of Judah" (Revelation 5:5). In fact, wrath is mentioned in the context of salvation. Paul says, "Since we have now been justified by his blood, how much more shall we be saved from God's wrath through him" (Romans 5:9). For as sinners "we were by nature objects of wrath. But because of his great love for us, God, who is rich in mercy, made us alive with Christ" (Ephesians 2:3-5). We are, therefore, admonished "to wait for his Son from heaven, whom he raised from the dead—Jesus, who rescues us from the coming wrath" (1 Thessalonians 1:10). "For God did not appoint us to suffer wrath but to receive salvation through our Lord Jesus Christ. He died for us" (1 Thessalonians 5:9, 10). Not until we realize what Christ has saved us from will we realize the wonder of the cross.

When we comprehend the cost of Calvary, we will understand Christ as our Substitute, our Salvation, and our Righteousness. Gazing long at the Crucified One transforms and fits us for heaven. By beholding, we are becoming changed (2 Corinthians 3:18). "Look and live," came the invitation to dying Jews in the desert (Numbers 21:4-9). They looked to the serpent on a pole and lived. Jesus said that serpent was a type of His crucifixion (John 3:14), for on the cross "God made him who had no sin to be sin for us, so that in him we might become the righteousness of God" (2 Corinthians 5:21). That death is our life. Nothing moves us like Calvary. Through Calvary, the love of Christ constrains us (2 Corinthians 5:14), so that we eagerly follow Him because we love Him (John 14:15). This is righteousness by faith lived out in love.

---

1. Ellen G. White, *The Signs of the Times*, 21 April 1890, 242 (2:378).
2. Ellen G. White, in her chapters "Why Was Sin Permitted?" (*Patriarchs and Prophets*, 33-43) and "The Origin of Evil" (*The Great Controversy*, 492-504), is clear that the supremacy of Christ and God's law are central to the controversy

(Legal Model), whereas the three basic questions relative to death (Great Controversy Trust-Healing Model) are not mentioned once in either chapter.

3. Ellen G. White, *The Signs of the Times*, 12 June 1901, 371 (4:185).

4. Ellen G. White, *The Signs of the Times*, 16 January 1893, 166 (3:13).

5. Ellen G. White, *The Advent Review and Sabbath Herald*, 13 October 1896, 631 (3:401).

6. Ellen G. White, *The Advent Review and Sabbath Herald*, 22 October 1895, 674 (3:302)

7. Ellen G. White, *The Signs of the Times*, 30 December 1889, 786 (2:345).

8. Ellen G. White, *The Advent Review and Sabbath Herald*, 10 March 1891, 115 (2:469).

9. Ellen G. White, *The Signs of the Times*, 16 April 1894, 372 (3:109).

10. Ellen G. White, *Advent Review and Sabbath Herald*, 22 October 1908, 7 (5:461).

11. Ellen G. White, *The Signs of the Times*, 2 October 1893, 742 (3:67).

12. Ellen G. White, *The Review and Herald*, 21 November 1912 (6:294).

13. Ellen G. White, *Advent Review and Sabbath Herald*, 16 March 1886, 162 (2:28).

14. Ellen G. White, *The Faith I Live By* (Hagerstown, Md.: Review and Herald, 1958), 50.

15. Ellen G. White, *Education*, 263.

16. Ellen G. White, *The Great Controversy*, 489.

17. Ellen G. White, *The Signs of the Times*, 14 May 1902, 306 (4:238).

18. Ibid.

19. Ellen G. White, *The Desire of Ages*, 762, 763.

20. Ellen G. White, *The Signs of the Times*, 5 February 1894, 212 (3:97).

21. Ellen G. White, *The Signs of the Times*, 31 July 1901 (4:192).

22. *The Desire of Ages*, 19, 20.

23. The GCTHM equates human need with that of unfallen angels—the sole need is revelation. But Scripture makes a distinction (Hebrews 2:14-18).

24. John R. W. Stott, *The Cross of Christ* (Downers Grove, Ill.: InterVarsity Press, 1986), 109.

25. *The Desire of Ages*, 762, 763.

Chapter 3

Christ
Our Only Restorer

David J. Murphy, a thirty-year-old lawyer in Chicago, received a phone call from an elderly woman in California. Annie Saucier, a widow, needed some legal work done for a small real-estate transaction in Chicago. Murphy did it for her, and because he thought she was destitute charged her a fraction of his normal fee. She called again about a title problem for an old house on Chicago's south side. Murphy took care of it and didn't send a bill. When Saucier's ninety-one-year-old brother died in Chicago, she asked the lawyer to bury him. He obliged and sent no bill. Saucier moved back to Chicago and had a stroke in the summer of 1984 at age eighty-two. She wanted Murphy to write her will. In it, she left him $140,000. When she died, Murphy did not take a penny. He distributed his share to family members who had helped Saucier.[1] Unselfishness—what a rare attribute! The supremely unselfish Lawyer is our ascended Saviour, who ever liveth to make intercession for us (Hebrews 7:25).

Christ's work for humankind didn't end at the cross. "After he had provided purification for sins, he sat down at the right hand of the Majesty in heaven" (Hebrews 1:3). Hebrews tells us that the place where Christ is seated is "in the sanctuary, the true tabernacle set up by the Lord, not by man" (Hebrews 8:2). Clearly, Christ went to the heavenly sanctuary. It was a place already in heaven at the time of His ascension.

The sanctuary in heaven

Throughout the Old Testament, mention is made of a heavenly sanctuary. Thus David said, "The Lord is in His holy temple, the Lord's throne is in heaven" (Psalms 11:4, Amplified Bible). Another psalmist confessed that God looks down "from the height of His sanctuary, from Heaven did the Lord behold the earth" (Psalms 102:19, Amplified Bible). Micah speaks of God witnessing "from his holy temple" (Micah 1:2).

God asked Moses to build a sanctuary "exactly like the pattern I will show you" (Exodus 25:9; compare verse 40). The pattern was either a miniature model or some blueprints. As Richard M. Davidson says, "If Moses had been shown merely architect's plans, it would seem likely that these plans would have been made available to take down from the mountain, so that the builders could follow them. But the record maintains that he brought down only the two tables of stone (Exodus 32:15)."[2] Moses was shown that the tabernacle was to have two rooms, the Holy Place and the Most Holy Place, with a curtain separating the two (Exodus 26:33, 34). The Jewish year had one Day of Atonement during which the high priest went into the Most Holy Place (Leviticus 15), and during each day of the year, including the Day of Atonement, the daily ministry was continuous (Hebrew *tamid*, e.g., Daniel 8:11).

Christ in the Holy Place of the heavenly sanctuary

Christ ascended to the throne to begin the first phase (the daily) of His ministry as High Priest in heaven's sanctuary. Revelation 4 and 5 give insight into His arrival and inauguration. John sees the Father seated on His throne with twenty-four elders seated on their thrones around the Father's throne (Revelation 4:3, 4). The scene includes worship of God as Creator (verses 10, 11). Then the scene changes. The Father is shown seated on the throne with a sealed scroll (Rev. 5:1, 7). The cry goes out, "Who is worthy to break the seals and open the scroll?" But no one was found worthy (verses 1-3).

John wept much because no one was worthy to open the scroll. "Then one of the elders said to me, 'Do not weep! See, the Lion of the tribe of Judah, the Root of David, has triumphed. He is able to open the scroll and its seven seal's" (verse 5). Then Christ comes to the Father and takes the scroll (verses 6, 7). The singing response is, 'Worthy is the Lamb, who was slain, to receive power and wealth and wisdom and strength and honor and glory and praise!' " (verse 12). This is the inauguration of Christ as High Priest.

How important is Christ's intercession?

First, think of the good news of Calvary. Whereas "the wages of sin is death, . . . the gift of God is eternal life in Christ Jesus our Lord" (Romans 6:23). Christ died for everyone (Hebrews 2:9). "We all, like sheep, have gone astray, each of us has turned to his own way; but the Lord has laid on him the iniquity of us all" (Isaiah 53:6). "God made him who had no sin to be sin for us, so that in him we might become the righteousness of God" (2 Corinthians 5:21).

"Christ was treated as we deserve, that we might be treated as He deserves. He was condemned for our sins, in which He had no share, that we might be justified by His righteousness, in which we had no share. He suffered the death which was ours, that we might receive the life which was His. 'With his stripes we are healed' [Isaiah 53:5]."[3] This is the ultimate in substitution. He took our place. This is an awesome exchange. "Christ died for our sins" (1 Corinthians 15:3). "He has appeared once for all at the end of the ages to do away with sin by the sacrifice of himself" (Hebrews 9:26). For "without the shedding of blood there is no forgiveness" (verse 22). This is wondrous good news, but if He paid human debt and forgave human sin on Calvary, why does He need to intercede for humankind?

The incredible thing is the importance of His intercession. "The intercession of Christ in man's behalf in the sanctuary above is as essential to the plan of salvation as was His death upon the cross."[4] How could anything be as essential as Calvary? Because in His intercession, Christ applies in human experience what He accomplished at the cross. There He died *for us*. Now He applies that *in us*. This involves a Godward and a humanward movement. The Godward movement is His intercession for humans before God. The humanward movement is His sending of blessing from God to humankind.

The Godward intercession

Does Christ need to intercede before the Father to change Him? Is this why He is the mediator between humankind and the Father (1 Timothy 2:5)? Is He our Advocate before the Father (Job 16:19)? Christ was transparent about this; "I am not saying that I will ask the Father on your behalf. No, the Father himself loves you" (John 16:26, 27). Jesus is not denying that He will intercede but simply explaining that His intercession is not for the purpose of convincing God to love us. He does not need to pray to the Father to change Him or to get Him to love human beings, because He already loves humankind. "For God so loved the world that he gave his one and only Son, that whoever believes in him shall not perish but have eternal life" (John 3:16). It is important that we realize each Member of the Trinity is equally the God of love (1 John 4:8, 17).

God the Father receives bad press on planet Earth. Many think of Him as an angry judge, one who sits in heaven recording human actions in minute detail so He can bring up their misdeeds in the judgment. They confine Him to their Old Testament picture with the law, wars, and bloodshed. By contrast, they see Jesus as the God of the New Testament, with its focus on grace. They wrench the two Testaments apart as if they belonged to two different members, of the Trinity.

Jesus rejected such a myopic view. He said it straight; "Anyone who has seen me has seen the Father" (John 14:9). Jesus knew the truth about God. There is no difference between the Members of the Trinity. In fact, Ellen G. White gives a remarkable insight into what would have happened if the Father had become human and lived on planet Earth instead of the Son. "Had God the Father come to our world and dwelt among us, humbling Himself, veiling His glory, that humanity might look upon Him, the history that we have of the life of Christ would not have been changed. . . . In every act of Jesus, in every lesson of His instruction, we are to see and hear and recognize God. In sight, in hearing, in effect, it is the voice and movement of the Father."[5] In fact, Ellen White says, "the heart of Christ is full of unutterable love toward every soul that comes to Him. . . . The love manifested in Christ reveals the parental character of the Father; for God suffered with Christ."[6] "There are many who have thought that the Father had no part in the sufferings of the Son; but this is a mistake."[7]

It is clear from His high-priestly prayer that Christ does intercede before the Father (John 17). This chapter tells us what Christ is saying to the Father in the heavenly sanctuary. He prays for His disciples. "Holy Father, protect them by the power of your name—the name you gave me—so that they may be one as we are one." "My prayer is not that you take them out of the world but that you protect them from the evil one." "Sanctify them by the truth; your word is truth" (John 17:11, 15, 17). Then this prayer extends to all subsequent disciples, for Christ continues, "My prayer is not for them alone. I pray also for those who will believe in me through their message, that all of them may be one, Father, just as you are in me and I am in you. May they also be in us so that the world may believe that you have sent me" (verses 20, 21). Jesus asks for protection, sanctification, and unity for His followers.

Christ longs for His followers to be with Him. "Father, I want those you have given me to be with me where I am" (verse 24). Until then, He says to the Father, "I have made you known to them, and will continue to make you known in order that the love you have for me may be in them and that I myself may be in them" (verse 26).

Why does Christ intercede with God?

We know that Jesus does not intercede to cause the Father to love the rebel race. So why does He intercede? Why is His intercession as essential as His death? There are a number of answers. First, although Christ abides in Christians (John 15:5), as does the Holy Spirit (Acts 9:17; Ephesians 5:18), no one comes to the Father except through Christ (John

14:6). Even though "the Holy Spirit . . . works upon our hearts," as "true believers," our best work is deficient. Even our obedience, penitence, prayers, and praise, "passing through the corrupt channels of humanity . . . are so defiled that unless purified by blood, they can never be of value with God."[8] Moreover, "unless the Intercessor, who is at God's right hand, presents and purifies all by His righteousness, it is not acceptable to God." In fact, "the merit of Jesus must be mingled with our prayers and efforts, or they are as worthless as was the offering of Cain."[9]

Second, Christ intercedes because Satan is bent on destroying the race, even though Calvary liberated it. Zechariah saw "Joshua the high priest standing before the angel of the Lord [Christ], and Satan standing at his right side to accuse him. The Lord said to Satan, 'The Lord rebuke you, Satan!' ' (Zechariah 3:1, 2). Here is a scene in the heavenly temple: Satan the accuser and Christ the One rebuking him. From outward appearances, Satan has the edge. For "Joshua was dressed in filthy clothes as he stood before the angel" (verse 3). In other words, Satan's charge against him seems true, for look at his clothes! Intercession involves the great controversy. Christ does not plead with the Father to get Him to love us, but He does stand up for His followers against Satan's accusations, and He provides His own life and death to substitute for their forgiven acts of sin and their sinful state.

Christ commands, " 'Take off his filthy clothes.' " Then he says to Joshua, " 'See, I have taken away your sin, and I will put rich garments on you' " (verse 4). Here is pictured Christ as the Restorer. He provides a rich garment in exchange for a filthy one. He is in the business of clothing repenting sinners. Forgiveness leads to restoration. This reminds us of the prodigal son, who came home from the far country and its pigsty. He was given the best robe by his father (Luke 15:21, 22). If the Son places the robe on Joshua, the Father places it on the prodigal. This is appropriate when we realize that the Father is just as forgiving and accepting of returning sinners as Christ. So Christ's intercession rebukes Satan and clothes sinners—both a consequence of Calvary.

The humanward intercession

The clothing of forgiven sinners is a part of this humanward ministry of Christ. So is His continuing manifestation of the Father to humankind (John 17:26). This side of His intercession involves sending the Holy Spirit. Christ promised in the upper room, just hours before His death, "I will ask the Father, and he will give you another Counselor [Comforter] to be with you forever—the Spirit of truth" (John 14:16). He adds, "I will not leave you as orphans; I will come to you" (verse 18). So He sends the Holy Spirit, and through the Holy Spirit God is present.

The Holy Spirit is Christ-centered in His mission and message. In the Incarnation, He caused the omnipresent Christ to become a speck in Mary in the inexplicable miracle and marvel of the virgin birth (Matthew 1:20). Since the Incarnation, Jesus has been confined in one human body. He gave up omnipresence forever in becoming a man. What an eternal sacrifice! "Cumbered with humanity, Christ could not be in every place personally. Therefore it was for their interest that He should go to the Father, and send the Spirit to be His successor on earth."[10] So in Pentecost, and its extension through history, the Holy Spirit brings Jesus Christ and makes Him omnipresent in a miracle just as inexplicable and marvelous as the Incarnation. So it is true that He is with His people till the end of the world (Matthew 28:20; Hebrews 13:5).

Did you know the Holy Spirit gets a new name in the New Testament? He is called "the Spirit of his Son" (Galatians 4:6), "the Spirit of Christ" (Romans 8:9; 1 Peter 1:11), and "the Spirit of Jesus Christ" (Philippians 1:19). This is because of His new function to bring Christ to be with His people. He also comes to glorify Christ and not Himself (John 15:26; 16:12-14). If the Holy Spirit lives only to bring glory to Jesus, will not Christians do the same when the Spirit indwells them? Paul did. He confessed, "For to me, to live is Christ" (Philippians 1:21). When Christ alone becomes the focus of living, then Satan will be rebuked, Christians will be sanctified, and church members will be united. This is restoration. For this, Christ intercedes.

1. Mike Royko, "An Honest Lawyer? in Chicago?," *Readers Digest*, December 1985, 123, 124.
2. Richard M. Davidson, *Typology in Scripture* (Berrien Springs, Mich.: Andrews University Press, 1981), 376.
3. *The Desire of Ages*, 25.
4. *The Great Controversy*, 489.
5. *That I May Know Him*, 338.
6. Ellen G. White, *The Advent Review and Sabbath Herald*, 17 March 1896, 162 (3:342).
7. Ellen G. White, *The Signs of the Times*, 25 November 1889, 706 (2:339).
8. Ellen G. White, *Selected Messages*, 1:344.
9. Ellen G. White, *The Review and Herald*, 4 July 1893, 1 (3:403).
10. *The Desire of Ages*, 669.

Chapter 4

Christ
Our Only Advocate

A father with two noisy boys came aboard the 4:05 train to New York. The unruly boys ran up and down the car, disturbing the peace. Finally, a passenger, who sat next to the father, could take it no more. "Sir, don't you realize your boys are a nuisance?" He glanced at the father's worried face.

"Yes, I guess they are," he sighed. "We've just come from the hospital where their mother died." Suddenly, the boys' behavior didn't matter anymore. Anguish overflowed the passenger. Now he understood. The boys, and their father, were trying to cope.

In life, only God knows all about us, but the pre-advent judgment will cause the universe to understand both Him and us better.

The pre-advent judgment

The second phase of the post-resurrection sanctuary doctrine is unique to Seventh-day Adventists. They find in Daniel 7 and 8, together with Revelation 14:6, 7, biblical evidence for a pre-advent judgment. They call this judgment "pre-advent," denoting its time; and "investigative," denoting its method.

Many of God's end-time saints consider the pre-advent judgment as anything but good news, even though the first angel's message places the judgment in the context of the "eternal gospel" (Revelation 14:7). They apparently consider the judgment apart from its relation to the little horn in Daniel and apart from its roots in the cross, its relation to Christ's intercession, and its outworking in Armageddon.

The everlasting gospel is the truth about Calvary. If "the sacrifice of Christ as an atonement for sin is the great truth around which all other truths cluster" and if "in order to be rightly understood and appreciated, every truth in the word of God, from Genesis to Revelation, must be studied in the light that streams from the cross of Calvary,"[1] then Calvary must give us insight into the pre-advent judgment. No subsequent judgment calls into question the judgment of Calvary, neither is it different from, nor does it add to, but only reveals and applies what was completed there.

Judgment day is revealed by Calvary.[2] Jesus said of the cross, "Now is the time for judgment on this world; now the prince of this world will be driven out" (John 12:31; compare Revelation 12:9-13). Calvary judgment means ultimate deliverance for God's people and destruction of their enemy. In the pre-advent judgment, it is God's people who are delivered (Daniel 7:22, 26, 27) and the little horn that is destroyed (Daniel 7:11-14; Revelation 19:11-21). This is the outworking in history of the double verdict of Calvary. Internal contextual evidence in Daniel, beyond chapter 7, seems also to support this double verdict. Thus, "deliverance" (shezib, Daniel 3:17,28; 6:20; nasal, Daniel 3:29; 6:16; malat, Daniel 12:1) of Daniel and his three friends, from the lions' den and the fiery furnace, gives insight into the eschatological deliverance of those who have their names written in the "book" (sepher, Daniel 12:1), which is the book used in the pre-advent judgment (Daniel 7:10). Escalation from local deliverances to a universal deliverance is involved.[3] The historical deliverances for God's people also include destruction of their enemies in both the fiery furnace (Daniel 3:22) and the lions' den (Daniel 6:24).[4] Likewise, the eschatological deliverance of the saints has its counterpart in the destruction of their enemy (little horn; Daniel 7:26, 27).[5]

What is the good news about the pre-advent judgment?

No New Testament book develops so completely the post-resurrection ministry of Christ as does Hebrews. Christ's intercession for His people is a part of Christ's better ministry as compared with that of Old Testament priests, even as His sacrifice was better than the multiple cultic sacrifices. Examination of the records (Daniel 7:10) is only one side of the judgment. The other is the intercession, or advocacy, of Christ (1 Timothy 2:5; 1 John 2:1). Christ is there in the presence of God on behalf of His people (Hebrews 9:24), where He is able to fully save, for He ever lives to intercede (Hebrews 7:25). We noted this ministry in the previous chapter, where we saw that it is part of Christ's work to restore His people. The intercession described in Zechariah 3 and Hebrews takes place at the same time as the pre-advent judgment.

The end-time remnant need to capture the full impact of Zechariah and Hebrews relative to the continuing intercession-advocacy of the conquering Christ during the pre-advent judgment. Their focus must be on Christ and not on themselves. Revelation is precise: in the judgment hour, the saints worship Christ as their Creator (Revelation 14:7), realizing that just as He brought them into this world, so only He can get them into the next world.[6] End-time saints are pictured as naked (Revelation 3:18), just like Adam and Eve at the fall (Genesis 3:10, 21). No fig leaves, or human works, can supply the need. Only the slain Lamb can supply the covering; only the robe of Christ's righteousness (Isaiah 61:10; Revelation 6:11), the wedding garment supplied by the Lord (Matthew 22:11, 12), will suffice. The prodigal son needs the best robe to cover his tattered rags (Luke 15:22).

The first angel's message is an invitation to focus on Christ rather than upon character; upon His judgment rather than ours; on His perfection rather than our perfection. It is a call to God's people to worship and glorify Christ in the judgment hour (Revelation 14:7). If some Seventh-day Adventists continue to focus on their own perfection, their own works, then they are no better than the little horn that deflects attention away from Christ to itself (Hebrews 8:9-12). How much longer will Christ delay His coming in order to let people give up on themselves and come only to Him? God is waiting for His people to be like Zechariah. For 150 years, He has waited for people to understand the essence of the gospel in this judgment hour. He waits for His people to look beyond judgment to an intercessor, to grasp the judgment as part of the everlasting gospel, to see judgment as a gift, just as Calvary is. That truth will set them free (John 8:32) to take the good news to a dying world. Christ waits for this, not willing for any to perish (2 Peter 3:9).

Saints pass the judgment because they are different from the little horn. They do not speak great words against Christ or magnify themselves or persecute the saints or think to change God's times and laws or put themselves in Christ's place, casting His truth to the ground (see Daniel 7 and 8). They reflect Christ in their living. Satan "presents their sins before them to discourage them. He is constantly seeking occasion against those who are trying to obey God. Even their best and most acceptable services he seeks to make appear corrupt. By countless devices, the most subtle and the most cruel, he endeavors to secure their condemnation. Man cannot meet these charges himself. In his sin-stained garments, confessing his guilt, he stands before God. But Jesus our Advocate presents an effectual plea in behalf of all who by repentance and faith have committed the keeping of their souls to Him. He pleads their cause and vanquishes their accuser by the mighty arguments of Calvary."[7]

Calvary is preeminent

We are now ready to penetrate the heart of what is underway in the pre-advent judgment, and for that matter, what will continue in the millennial and postmillennial judgments (Revelation 20:7-15). God does not need the judgments, because He is omniscient (Psalms 33:13-15; 56:8; 104:24; 139:2, 6; 147:4; Isaiah 44:28; 46:9, 10; Malachi 3:16; Matthew 10:29, 30; Acts 15:8; Romans 11:33; Ephesians 3:10). "The Lord knows those who are his" (2 Timothy 2:19). He holds these judgments for the sake of created beings.[8] In the pre-advent judgment, the universe is looking at the records of human works, good and bad (Daniel 7:10). But more than that, they are looking to see whether individuals have accepted or rejected the saving work that Jesus did for them on the cross.[9] Their relation to the substitutionary judgment of the covenant Saviour determines whether they are saved and live with Him or are lost (compare John 16:26, 27; 17:3).

It is precisely that, and nothing else, that determines personal destiny. God is not asking us to be preoccupied with our perfection, but with His. It is His garment of righteousness that we need. So the pre-advent judgment is Christ-centered, not people-centered.[10] Human works are considered in the judgment. We do reap what we sow (Galatians 6:7). Yet it is not so much what individuals have or have not done that is decisive.[11] Rather, it is whether they have accepted or rejected what Christ has done for them when He was judged in their place at the cross (John 12:31).

It is also true that the judgment has as much to do with vindication of God as with the vindication of His followers. It provides proof to the universe that God is just. It shows why some will go to heaven and others will not. In this qualified sense, it is "the hour of *his* judgment" (Revelation 14:7). If God wants to open Himself up for investigation, then that is His choice. He does it to win the trust of the redeemed and the unfallen beings so that sin will never arise again. So the judgment is for the benefit of all created beings as well as for God's human followers. This is the breadth of the eternal-gospel context of the judgment. So the judgment is just as good news as the gospel!

The judgment does not repudiate Calvary. It is the Crucified who intercedes for us. The pre-advent judgment is part of the unfolding in salvation history of what was accomplished at the cross. Calvary moves inexorably to the deliverance of God's people and the destruction of their enemies, because both were accomplished by Christ on the cross. It is by the authority of Calvary that Christ delivers His saints and destroys Satan and all their other enemies in the coming battle of Armageddon (Revelation 19:14-21; 20:11-15). This will be the pre-advent implementation of the judgment verdict.

We need to fully understand Satan's scheme. What he has done on a general level, in deflecting attention from the authentic heavenly sanctuary service to his counterfeit earthly priesthood (little horn), he is doing on the personal level by deflecting attention away from humankind's only Substitute to humans themselves. Whether we look to an earthly priesthood or to our own righteousness for salvation, the problem is the same: Our gaze has been deflected away from Christ.

There is wondrous good news in the pre-advent judgment. For it does not stand by itself. It is surrounded by Calvary before it, Christ's intercession in it, and Armageddon beyond it. In all three events, Christ works consistently for His people and against their enemies. (This is why the little horn is investigated in the judgment and receives the judgment verdict at the battle of Armageddon.) In all three events, Christ is "the same yesterday and today and forever" (Hebrews 13:8). What Christ accomplished on the cross is now unfolding in all subsequent salvation history, including the pre-advent judgment. This is why the "hour of his judgment" is part of the "eternal gospel" (Revelation 14:6, 7). In this judgment hour, it is our crucified Saviour who "is able to save completely those who come to God through him, because he always lives to intercede for them" (Hebrews 7:25).

---

1. Ellen G. White, *Gospel Workers*, 315.

2. Scholars rightly find in Calvary the antitype of the typical Day of Atonement (Leviticus 16), but almost all fail to see further correspondence in a pre-advent judgment. Once the additional correspondence is seen, the implications of the cross to understanding the pre-advent judgment need to be explored.

3. Consider the deliverance from Babylonian captivity, after the seventy years, as a type of the call to come out of Babylon in Revelation 14 and 18.

4. If looked at sequentially, the destruction came first, before the deliverance, in the fiery-furnace incident, and the order was reversed in the lions' den experience. Although the typology should not be overly pushed, there is correspondence in the double result of "deliverance-destruction" between these two historical events and the result of the pre-advent judgment. It would appear that these historical events give some insight into the result of the apocalyptic pre-advent judgment, which is climaxed in the deliverance of the saints and the destruction of their enemies in Daniel 12:1 (compare Revelation 16–19).

5. Hans LaRondelle rightly sees that "the historical narratives of Daniel's own experiences in Babylon and Persia carry also typological significance for the end time" (*Journal of the Evangelical Theological Society*, 32:3, 1989, 345. See Hans LaRondelle, *Chariots of Salvation* (Hagerstown, Md.: Review and Herald, 1987), 155-157.

6. Compare Ellen G. White's first vision, in which she saw that only those who kept their eyes on Jesus made it up the path to heaven. Those taking their

gaze away from Him fell to the world below (*Early Writings*, 14).

7. Ellen G. White, *Testimonies for the Church*, 5:471.

8. All nonhuman created beings, plus the few human representatives in heaven (including Enoch, Elijah, Moses, and the twenty-four elders of Revelation 4, 5), witness the pre-advent investigation. All the redeemed witness the millennial investigation, and all the lost witness the post-millennial judgment. In this way, all intelligent created beings participate in the evaluation of God's judgments and find Him to be just (Revelation 15:3). The great-controversy questions about the justice of God are thus answered.

9. This involves clinging not only to Calvary but to the Crucified's continuing intercession, which is a result of the cross.

10. If the judgment is merely looking at what people have done, and the scriptural principle "by beholding we become changed" is applied (see 2 Corinthians 3:18), then a millennium of poring over bad works would be dangerous. I believe that the judgments have far more to do with observing how patiently Christ has worked for each person and where each turned Him down and so is far more Christ-centered than human-centered. Such an investigation is uplifting—it tells us more about the character of Christ than about the characters of fallen humans. To behold Christ's working will change us for the better, whereas to wallow in the morass of human sin would have the opposite effect.

11. Throughout eternity, "both the redeemed and the unfallen beings will find in the cross of Christ their science and their song" (*The Desire of Ages*, 19, 20.) We will come to understand in ever greater detail the depths of that gift and thereby receive greater revelation of God's love, where justice and mercy met. However, the 144,000 will "follow the Lamb wherever he goes" (Revelation 14:4), perhaps to tell their experience of living beyond probation's close, when they experienced spiritual and physical deliverance. They sing "the song of Moses and the Lamb—a song of deliverance. None but the hundred and forty-four thousand can learn that song; for it is the song of their experience—an experience such as no other company have ever had" (*The Great Controversy*, 649). Two pages later, *The Great Controversy* says, "The cross of Christ will be the science and the song of the redeemed through all eternity" (651). The song of the Lamb (cross) has a stanza called the "song of Moses and the Lamb." The experience of the 144,000 is the final outworking of the cross in human lives during the pre-advent judgment and before Christ returns.

Chapter 5

Christ
Our Only Refuge

Jogging at nine thousand feet in the Colorado Rockies tested stamina. A small group kept up the pace. Winding our way through the giant pines, the pathway seemed to stretch on forever. Then, fifteen minutes into the run, I needed to return to pack in order to catch a flight and started back alone. All went well until things began to be confusing. Which way had we come? Which turn should I take? I thought I had it down, but evidence proved contrary. Nothing but endless trees suffocatingly close, with no way out beyond them. I longed for streets, houses, anything but trees!

Finally, I made my way to a higher place, climbed up, and looked. Only trees to the horizon throughout 360 degrees! My heart sank. My knees felt weak. My mind raced. *There's no building in sight. Where did I come from? How can I get back? What if I don't?* I could almost see the newspaper headline: "Gulley found dead after search." I knew I had to snap out of that way of thinking. I staggered over to a large rock face, leaned against it, and poured out my heart to Christ. I felt so helpless.

Two more times I climbed to high points. Finally, from the second promontory, the sea of trees was interrupted in one place by part of a fire-observation tower. "Thank You, Lord!" I burst out, "Maybe that was the one I visited yesterday. Please help me keep a bearing on it from the winding pathway in the trees below." That was extremely difficult. Have you ever tried to keep your bearings while navigating a trail

45

that seems to have been made for snakes?

Eventually, I made my way to the tower. To me, it was the most beautiful building I had ever seen. You understand what I mean. It was a reference point. How important to have a reference point. So many wander aimlessly through life, not knowing where they are going. Like a ship at sea without chart or compass, they lack a reference point. One important reference point is God's law.

The nature of God's law

God's law is a limited manifestation of what God is like. It is an expression of His very being. In principle, it is as eternal as He is and transcends any human effort to change it.

Law as a transcript of God's character

God's "law is without variableness, unalterable, eternal, because it is the transcript of His character."[1] " 'God is love . . . His nature, His law, is love. It ever has been; it ever will be. 'The high and lofty One that inhabiteth eternity,' 'whose ways are everlasting,' changeth not. With Him 'is no variableness, neither shadow of turning.' "[2]

The unchanging God (Malachi 3:6) gives expression of Himself in His unchanging law (Matthew 5:18; Luke 16:17). One can no more change His law than change God. Both God and His law transcend created beings in such a way that they function, in different ways, to change human beings rather than be changed by them.

God's attributes and the law's inherent qualities are the same. Scripture says (1) God is righteous (Ezra 9:15), and so is the law (Psalms 119:172); (2) God is perfect (Matthew 5:48), and so is the law (Psalms 19:7); (3) God is holy (Leviticus 19:2), and so is the law (Romans 7:12); (4) God is good (Psalms 34:8), and so is the law (Romans 7:12); and (5) God is truth (Deuteronomy 32:4), and so is the law (Psalms 119:142).[3]

Law as revelation of the Trinity

"God is love" (1 John 4:8, 16). He is also eternal (Psalms 90:2; Revelation 1:8). Before They gave life to the first created being, the Trinity lived together in a love relationship, in which each loved the others supremely. They loved God, and as such, loved their fellow beings. The very essence of this experience is revealed in the Ten Commandments, which Christ said are summed up as love to God and love to humankind (Matthew 22:37-40).

Law as spiritual

"God is spirit, and his worshipers must worship in spirit and in truth" (John 4:24). Like its Author, "the law is spiritual" (Romans 7:14). Jesus showed the spiritual depths of the law in the Sermon on the Mount (Matthew 5-7). He said the law penetrates the outward performance to what lies behind it, such as anger (Matthew 5:21, 22) and lust (verses 27, 28). One can break the law in the mind, without ever committing an overt act. Like Scripture, the law penetrates to "the thoughts and attitudes of the heart" (Hebrews 4:12). In fact, the tenth commandment, against covetousness, concerns only the mind (Exodus 20:17).

Law as positive

The law seems negative with its "You shall nots." But in the context of love to God, these apparent negatives become positives. Jesus said, "If you love me, you will obey what I command" (John 14:15). Apply this to the Ten Commandments and they say, "If you love me, you will not" kill, steal, etc. They become promises. Also, as pointed out in *Seventh-day Adventists Believe*, "the sixth commandment, 'You shall not kill,' has as its positive side 'You shall promote life' " (235).

The purpose of the Ten Commandments

God gave the Ten Commandments to Israel after He delivered them from the Egyptians at the Red Sea. It was Christ who led them through the waters and destroyed their enemies. He was the One who gave the Ten Commandments to Moses on Mount Sinai. He said, "I am the Lord your God, who brought you out of Egypt, out of the land of slavery. You shall have no other gods before me" (Exodus 20:2, 3). The Ten Commandments were given by the One who had just saved them in the greatest deliverance recorded in Old Testament history.

Not just rules

It is important to see that the Ten Commandments were not just rules given by a distant God, One who dictates to humankind from heaven. He had been with them in the Red Sea (Exodus 14:19). Just as He worked there for their good, so He spoke the Ten Commandments for their good (Exodus 20:1-17). The commandments are no more capricious or arbitrary than His deliverance.

For protection

Properly understood, the Ten Commandments deliver human beings from many heartaches. For example, stealing, adultery, and murder all have obvious consequences. The commandments act as a hedge of protection from these consequences. They are a refuge from sinning and its heartaches. They provide minimum boundaries. Those who do not break the laws have no fear from the condemnation of the law. "God's law is given to men as a hedge, a shield. Whoever accepts its principles is preserved from evil."[4] No wonder Christ could say, "If you want to enter life, obey the commandments" (Matthew 19:17).

For freedom

"Everyone who sins breaks the law; in fact, sin is lawlessness" (1 John 3:4). "Everyone who sins is a slave to sin" (John 8:34). By contrast, when Christ dwells within the Christian, He "is able to keep you from falling [sinning] and to present you before his glorious presence without fault and with great joy" (Jude 24). This is freedom from sin. Christ delivers people from slavery to the lower nature and frees them to fellowship with Him, and through Him, with their fellow humans (Matthew 22:37-40). For, "Where the Spirit of the Lord is, there is freedom" (2 Corinthians 3:17). The psalmist discovered this fact and exclaimed, "I will walk about in freedom, for I have sought out your precepts" (Psalms 119:45). No wonder the law is called "the perfect law that gives freedom" (James 1:25).

For love

A Pharisee, an expert in the law, asked Jesus "which is the greatest commandment in the Law?" (see Matt. 22:34-36). "Jesus replied: 'Love the Lord your God with all your heart and with all your soul and with all your mind.' This is the first and greatest commandment. And the second is like it: 'Love your neighbor as yourself.' All the Law and the Prophets hang on these two commandments' " (verses 37-40).

These two principles, basic to all of God's laws, are the purpose behind all Scripture, and they sum up the Ten Commandments. The first four commandments deal with our relationship to God (Exodus 20:1-11), and the last six instruct us in how to relate to our fellow human beings (verses 12-17). To love God supremely and one's neighbor as oneself is to live the very essence of the law. The order is important. Love to God frees one to love humankind.

For Christlikeness

The same Christ who gave freedom from Egyptian slavery to Israel and delivered them from the Egyptians in the Red Sea longs to deliver His people from slavery to themselves, release them from sin's dominion over them, and free them to love as He does. He said, "A new command I give you: Love one another. As I have loved you, so you must love one another" (John 13:34).

How to keep the Ten Commandments

When it comes to the law, we need to see the truth as it is in Jesus. The law speaks of a relationship with God. This relationship is not the result of law keeping, but it is necessary for law keeping. Without Christ, the children of Israel could never have gained freedom from the Egyptians (Exodus 14:13, 14; 15:1, 2). Similarly, without Christ, there is no law keeping (John 15:5). For it is human nature to break the law. Apart from Christ, we say with Paul, "What I want to do I do not do, but what I hate I do. . . . I know that nothing good lives in me, that is, in my sinful nature. For I have the desire to do what is good, but I cannot carry it out" (Romans 7:15, 18). Paul delights in the law (verse 22), but the law of sin works within him. "What a wretched man I am! Who will rescue me from this body of death?" (verse 24).

Jesus said, " If a man remains in me and I in him, he will bear much fruit; apart from me you can do nothing" (John 15:5). Abiding in Christ enables one to keep His law. It is the love of Christ constraining the Christian that keeps the law (2 Corinthians 5:14). It is Christ, who keeps the Christian, who enables the Christian to keep the law (Jude 24).

Christ lived the law

On one occasion, Jesus said, "Do not think that I have come to abolish the Law or the Prophets; I have not come to abolish them but to fulfill them. I tell you the truth, until heaven and earth disappear, not the smallest letter, not the least stroke of a pen, will by any means disappear from the Law until every-thing is accomplished" (Matthew 5:17, 18). The law is the To-rah, or sum total, of God's revealed will. In Jesus' day, the law and the prophets were recognized as two sections of the Old Testament (Matthew 7:12, 11:13; 22:40; Luke 16:16; 24:44). Jesus is concerned about the law, or God's will. He came to do the Father's will. "He said, 'Here I am, I have come to do your will'" (Hebrews 10:9). Moreover, Christ said, "I have come down from heaven not to do my will but to do the will of him who sent me" (John 6:38).

Christ fulfilled the moral law by living the principles of the law in His love for God and for humanity. He came with love for God and humanity. He came to do His Father's will. Such love fired His mission. He did not come to destroy the law. How could He destroy His love by loving? His entire life exemplified what loving God and loving humans means. It means being willing to go to the cross for the undeserving. When Jesus, on Calvary, hung helpless, lonely, and hated, He took all the mock-ery, jeers, taunts, and rejection, and instead of hurling them back, turned to His Father, pleading, "Father, forgive them."

He sank to the lowest depths that any human can. Taking our place as a sinner, He plunged into hell.

Dying as a sinner, He hung between heaven and earth—lonely between His God and humankind. "My God, my God, why have you forsaken me?" (Matthew 27:46), forced from quivering lips in the face of blatant rejection by people—Roman soldiers, His church, and even His disciples. No voice from heaven pierced His gloom, just as no follower stood up to defend Him. It seemed that all but the dying thieves remained silent. By sheer faith, and in unswerving love for God and humanity, He endured this bitter agony. As He hung there, He gave the greatest demonstration of the law's eternal principles. He would rather die than break His relationship with either God or humankind. In fact, He died because He maintained that double love relationship in spite of being subjected to its very opposite.

Any suggestion that the cross changed the law stems from a superficial understanding of what took Jesus to and kept Him on that wood. If there was any way God could have saved the world and spared His Son this utter ignominy and devastating anguish, He would have done it. But salvation's plan is love for the undeserving—the outpouring of the very heart of the law as expressed in love. It is loving the unworthy, loving them for their sake and not for one's own sake. "God is love" means He went to the cross willingly in an utter self-abandonment for others—a naked selflessness that opens up the very meaning of the law.

Christ our only Refuge

Recently, I walked along the path at Peak's Point in Hong Kong. What a spectacular view, looking way down over the skyscrapers, with a vast panorama over the South China Sea, the airport, and the mountains and ocean beyond. At one place, there was nothing between me and that vast vista except a rail. Climbing on the narrow path to heaven, the law is like that rail. It warns of the dangers in the journey. To go beyond it into sin means death. The law is a boundary, and as such, a reference point.

Ellen G. White's first vision was of the remnant church making its way up the steep path that leads to the heavenly kingdom. It is a narrow way. We might say that the hedge of the law gives boundaries to keep the travelers safe on the path. By contrast, the way that leads to eternal death is broad, for it has no protecting hedge of the law. People are falling downward to perdition. In her vision of the narrow way, she noticed that some fell to the world below. But of another group, she assured us: "If they kept their eyes fixed on Jesus, who was just before them, leading them to the city, they were safe."[5]

The law is like the stoplight at an intersection. It is there for our safety, to keep us from an accident. When it is red, it means stop. Green means go. The stoplight tells us what to do at the intersection. But it cannot do anything if we have an accident. Just so, the law cannot save sinful humans. Only Christ can.

Christ is our only Refuge on the journey. For He does not just meet us at intersections; He travels the journey with us. He is the only One who keeps us from falling (Jude 24). On the upward journey, the eyes are kept on Christ and not on His law. In Beijing, China, I walked up a very steep place in the famous China Wall. To do so, I kept looking above and at the steps, rather than looking to the walls on each side of the path. The law is for our protection, but looking at Christ is our only refuge. We do not keep the law to be saved but because we are saved. Or, as Jesus expressed it, "If you love me, you will obey what I command" (John 14:15).

When you love someone, it is easy to respond to their wishes. I have a friend who used to hate the color green in clothes until he met his sweetheart, who looks so good in green. Loving her made all the difference. There are believers who try to keep the law without first loving Christ. Their lives remain empty. They work hard. They struggle to obey. Perhaps, at times, like the Pharisee, they say, "Thank God I am not like this sinner," referring to a fellow church member.

Some will be shocked at the second advent. They will be rejected. "Why, we have preached in Your name, performed miracles for You, and done many good things. We have kept the law," they will protest. But Jesus will reply sadly, "I never knew you. Away from me, you evildoers!" (Matthew 7:23; compare Luke 13:24-27). Even supposedly good works apart from Christ are evil! Knowing Christ personally is the only way to eternal life (John 17:3).

Christ knocks at Laodicea's door because He longs to come in to fill the void and give joy to the life and freedom to the soul. Where He is, there is heaven on earth. Where He is, people delight to keep the law. Where He is, there is support for the journey. Where He is, there is no fear of the coming crisis. Where He is, there is assurance of salvation. Where He is, there is true law keeping as a love response for His keeping the law, His love to God and to humanity, when He hung there lonely, misunderstood, and hated on the cross.

Christ is our only Refuge from law breaking. He is our only Refuge from self, from Satan, from peer pressures to join the world. Christ will be our only Refuge when the Sunday-law test comes with such overwhelming power upon the remnant church. Only Christ can keep us true when that day arrives. Only Christ can deepen our hunger for Him and for His Word. We receive Christ through His Word. He comes within as we take His Word within. Then we can say in freedom, "I have hidden your word in my heart that I might not sin against you" (Psalms 119:11). That is true law keeping.

---

1. Ellen G. White, *The Signs of the Times*, 12 March 1896.
2. Ellen G. White, *Patriarchs and Prophets*, 33.
3. General Conference of Seventh-day Adventists Ministerial Association, *Questions on Doctrine* (Hagerstown, Md.: Review and Herald, 1957), 129.
4. Ellen G. White, *Education*, 76, 77.
5. Ellen G. White, *Early Writings*, 14.

Chapter 6

Christ
Our Only Rest

The Great Wall of China protected the Chinese for centuries. Yet three times barbarians broke through into China. The wall remained an adequate protection. But the gatekeepers were bribed. Satan has bribed angels and humans, but the wall of God's law still remains unchanged.

Sin originated in one bent on changing the law and disputing Christ's supremacy (Isaiah 14:12-15; Ezekiel 28:13-15). "In heavenly council the angels pleaded with Lucifer. The Son of God presented before him the greatness, the goodness, and the justice of the Creator, and the sacred, unchanging nature of His law."[1] What was his response? "While secretly fomenting discord and rebellion, he with consummate craft caused it to appear as his sole purpose to promote loyalty and to preserve harmony and peace."[2]

There are two focuses that will occupy us in this chapter: (1) Satan's attack on the Sabbath as a part of His attack on Christ, packaged in a Christian guise, and (2) the essence of the Sabbath as teaching "the distinction between the Creator and His creatures."[3] This meaning of the Sabbath is unfolded more and more as we move through the Bible.

Sunday is presented by major thinkers in church history as a day in honor of Christ's resurrection. It is clothed in a Christian garb. It allegedly honors Christ's resurrection.

Satan's crafty plan
Satan craftily clothes his attack on Christ in a Christian

guise. How inexplicable! His very life and all he had came from Christ. He held the place of highest honor among created beings. He stood as the covering cherub at the throne (Ezekiel 28:14). Yet Lucifer plunged down a path that led inexorably to Calvary. He would kill the One who gave him life. He would go on, in the Christian age, to overthrow the Sabbath, which reminds humans of their Creator (Exodus 20:11). Satan's whole rebellion is Christ-centered. Calvary and Sunday expose his hatred of Christ. Sunday is Satan's creation, not a day in honor of Christ's resurrection. Whether realized or not, Sunday honors Satan's work of attempting to change God's commandment rather than Christ's resurrection. Sunday observance is Satan's commandment to replace the Sabbath command of the preincarnate Christ (Deuteronomy 5:22).

Change of seventh-day Sabbath predicted

The Bible prophesied that a power that speaks against God and oppresses His saints would try to change the time and the law (Daniel 7:25). Clearly, the only *time* mentioned in the law is the seventh-day Sabbath. Thus it is clear that Daniel's prophecy predicted a power that is against God would attempt to change the seventh-day Sabbath. The change to Sunday is the only one attempted by a so-called Christian church.

Change of seventh-day Sabbath admitted

The recent *Catechism of the Catholic Church* (1994) speaks about "The Sunday obligation" as a "precept of the Church" in section 2180. Section 2181 reads, "The Sunday Eucharist is the foundation and confirmation of all Christian practice. . . . Those who deliberately fail in this obligation commit a grave sin."[4] In the 1977 edition of *The Convert's Catechism of Catholic Doctrine*, a couple of questions help us understand just how Satan has tampered with God's law. "Question: Which is the Sabbath day? Answer. Saturday is the Sabbath day. Question. Why do we observe Sunday instead of Saturday? Answer. We observe Sunday instead of Saturday because the Catholic Church transferred the solemnity from Saturday to Sunday."[5]

Christ's name in the Sabbath

Jesus said of Himself, "The Son of Man is Lord of the Sabbath" (Luke 6:5), and the fourth commandment calls it "the sabbath of the Lord thy God" (Exodus 20:10, KJV). An attack against the Sabbath is an attack against Christ. It is also an attack against all that the Sabbath represents. The Sabbath is a memorial of Christ's creation (verse 11), His liberation (Deuteronomy 5:15), and His relationship with His followers (Ezekiel 20:12). Setting up a substitute Sabbath (Sunday) is the work of a substitute Christ (Satan). This is the bottom line. Satan hates Christ, wants to overthrow Him and wrench His rule from Him. Part of his strategy is to promote Sunday as the Christian Sabbath. In the end, he will go so far as to attempt to counterfeit the second coming in order to promote Sunday sacredness. This will be his ultimate attack against Christ and His day.

Doctrines of men

The scribes and Pharisees changed God's doctrines too. Though they did not change the day of worship, they made the Sabbath a day of drudgery. Any alteration of truth is opposed by Christ. He said, "In vain they worship Me, teaching as doctrines the commandments of men" (Matthew 15:9, NKJV).

The Sabbath unfolded throughout Scripture

The meaning of the Sabbath is added to as one goes through biblical history.

Christ rested on Creation Sabbath

All the universe was created by the Father through the Son (John 1:3; Colossians 1:16; Hebrews 1:2). Christ is the Creator. He rested from His creation work and "blessed the seventh day and made it holy" (Genesis 2:3). Nowhere in Scripture is the holiness of the seventh day rescinded, nor is it transferred to another day. Creation Sabbath was the first full day of life for Adam and Eve. This Sabbath was a day to celebrate the finished creative work of Christ. It was Christian through and through.

The fourth commandment

At Mount Sinai, Christ gave the law to Israel. The fourth commandment asked them to "remember the Sabbath day by keeping it holy," refraining from the secular work of the six days, "for in six days" Christ created everything, rested on the Sabbath day, and blessed it (Exodus 20:8-11). The Sabbath is clearly linked to Creation, with the request "Remember" suggesting that it had been kept before this giving of the Ten Commandments. In fact, twice as much manna fell on the sixth day so that the Sabbath could be kept, and this preceded the lawgiving on Mount Sinai (Exodus 16:4, 5).

The second giving of the law

After receiving the two law tables, Moses descended the mountain and saw the Israelites dancing around a golden calf. He threw the tables down in righteous indignation, and they broke. God called Moses to come up the mountain again to have the tables rewritten. This time, due to the false god (golden calf) experience, the purpose of the Sabbath was extended. "Remember that you were slaves in Egypt and that the Lord your God brought you out of there with a mighty hand and an outstretched arm. Therefore the Lord your God has commanded you to observe the Sabbath day" (Deuteronomy 5:15).

Whereas the Sabbath had celebrated the finished work of Christ's creation, now His finished work of liberation in the Exodus became a further event for Sabbath celebration. Both experiences were equally a gift from Christ. He gave them life without their help. He rescued them through the Red Sea without their help, even though they cooperated with Him by walking across.

The Sabbath as a sign

By the time we come to Ezekiel's ministry, Judah is in Babylonian captivity. They are far from the Holy Land home. Christ says of their ancestors, they utterly "desecrated my Sabbaths," for "their hearts were devoted to their idols" (Ezekiel 20:16). He reminds them, "I gave them my Sabbaths as a sign between us, so they would know that I the Lord made them holy" (verse 12). God intended that the Sabbath would celebrate the work of sanctification that Christ is accomplishing. Sanctification is a setting apart, a making holy. Just as the Sabbath is set apart from the other six days, so God's Sabbath keepers are set apart from the world. Just as Christ made the Sabbath holy, so He makes His people holy. Creation, the Exodus, and sanctification are all gifts of Christ that the Sabbath celebrates.

Christ and the Sabbath

Christ began His ministry on a Sabbath (Luke 4:16), proclaiming His mission to set the oppressed and prisoners free and to announce "the year of the Lord's favor" (Luke 4:18, 19). Christ cited Isaiah 61:1, 2, claiming that "today this scripture is fulfilled in your hearing" (Luke 4:21).

1. Christ as a Sabbath keeper

Christ kept the Sabbath as part of Creation week (Genesis 2:3) and during His life on earth (Mark 1:21; Luke 4:16). He did not keep the Sabbath because He was a Jew, even though this can be said about His being circumcised and keeping the Passover. Rather, He kept the Sabbath as He kept all the Ten Commandments. In this, He is an example for all humans, and not just for Jews.

2. Sabbath given to humankind

Christ said, "The Sabbath was made for man, not man for the Sabbath" (Mark 2:27). Christ did not say the Sabbath was made for the Jewish race, but for humankind. Clearly, Christ rejected the national confines placed on the Sabbath by human thinkers and placed it into its global context.

3. Christ's mission to set prisoners free

Christ identified His mission with the essence of the Sabbath. He had come to bring rest to sin-sick, weary people. He had come to set them free in Himself. He would demonstrate through miracles the total freedom He had to offer. And He often chose a Sabbath to perform that healing (Luke 4:31-40; 13:10-17; Matthew 12:9-21; John 5:1-18; 9:1-41) so that the physical release could give some insight into the spiritual salvation He came to give. Christ gave the Sabbath and salvation to humankind. He illustrated the salvation gift through the Sabbath miracles.

The Sabbath gift of freedom had deteriorated into a day of work in Christ's day. There were some six hundred *halakah*, or man-made requirements, that smothered the day with legalistic burdens. The Sabbath was no longer an invitation to set the burdened free. It had become itself an instrument to shackle.

4. Crucifixion Sabbath

Sabbath celebrates Christ's finished work of creation, His finished work of deliverance at the Red Sea, and His finished work of salvation payment at the cross. If the first Sabbath was a celebration by a couple, the Exodus Sabbath celebration was for a nation, and the crucifixion Sabbath celebration was for a universe.

Did you ever wonder why Christ died on a Friday? Creation Friday and crucifixion Friday have something in common. They are both the end of a process—the end of creation and the end of Christ's sacrifice to pay for human sin. When He cried out from the cross, "It is finished" (John 19:30), the payment had been paid in full. Both Fridays were also the beginning for the human race. It was on Creation Friday that the race had an Adam (Genesis 1:26, 27). It was on crucifixion Friday that the race had a new Adam (compare Romans 5:15-19; 1 Corinthians 15:45-49).

The perpetuity of the Sabbath

The secondary meaning of Hebrews 4 is that there still remains a seventh-day Sabbath rest (*katapausis*) for the people of God (verses 4, 5), and Hebrews was written in AD 70, nearly forty years after Christ's crucifixion and resurrection. Hebrews 4 denies the possibility of the Sabbath's demise or change. Hebrews 4 agrees with Christ's linking of the Sabbath with the entire human race.

The Jerusalem Conference (Acts 15:1-29) is the first recorded "General Conference" committee of the early church. They discussed things that were Jewish and not necessary to continue in the Christian church, such as circumcision. If God wanted to change the Sabbath, this would have been a perfect time to make it known. The silence is eloquent. After all, Christ had given many admonitions during His ministry, but never once did He speak of changing the Sabbath. No wonder the Sabbath will be kept forever, according to Isaiah (Isaiah 66:22, 23)!

How to prepare for the coming Sunday-law crisis

Satan will come as Christ and promote Sunday, and this will be an almost overmastering delusion. Only a few will stand against a world that complies (Revelation 13:3). How will they be able to do this?

Need to experience the Sabbath rest

To survive the Sabbath test, we need to experience the Sabbath rest: The Sabbath test is far more than mathematics. It transcends which day is the seventh. It goes to the essence of the Sabbath itself. The Sabbath teaches *"the distinction between the Creator and His creatures."*[6] This is precisely what Satan has refused to acknowledge since the inception of his rebellion. In the end-time, Satan seeks to replace his Creator when he comes impersonating Christ and promoting Sunday. The end-time saints will not worry about the worldwide opposition against them. This is because Sabbath keeping is more than a day—it is an experience. They keep Christ's Sabbath and so can rest in Him. They experience the Sabbath resting in a Creator who alone can take them through.

Need to rest in Christ

Just as Christ came to set the captives free in His day, so He longs to set the captives free in our time. So many are afraid of coming events. To these He offers, "Come to me, all you who are weary and burdened, and I will give you rest. Take my yoke upon you and learn from me, for I am gentle and humble in heart, and you will find rest for your souls. For my yoke is easy and my burden is light" (Matthew 11:28-30).

We rest in Him as our Creator-Redeemer. Psalm 91 speaks of this rest during final events on planet Earth. "He who dwells in the shelter of the Most High will rest in the shadow of the Almighty. I will say of the Lord, 'He is my refuge and my fortress, my God, in whom I trust.' Surely he will save you from the fowler's snare and from the deadly pestilence. He will cover you with his feathers, and under his wings you will find refuge; his faithfulness will be your shield and rampart. You will not fear the terror of night, nor the arrow that flies by day, nor the pestilence that stalks in the darkness, nor the plague that destroys at midday. A thousand may fall at your side, ten thousand at your right hand, but it will not come near you. You will only observe with your eyes and see the punishment of the wicked. If you make the Most High your dwelling, even the Lord, who is my refuge—then no harm will befall you, no disaster will come near your tent" (verses 1-10).

Sabbath keeping is being kept by Christ

Not until we realize the distinction between ourselves and our Creator, until we find nothing in ourselves to commend us to Him and to fit us for heaven, will we really rest in Him. Resting in Him is the heart of the gospel. It is the good news that in Him alone is our title and fitness for heaven.[7] Having done all good things, we are still unprofitable servants (Luke 17:10). Gone is confidence in works, in position and title. We have become as little children (Matthew 18:3)—trusting in Christ alone. Sabbath keeping is more than keeping a day; it is being kept by Christ in that day. It is a day that reminds us He means everything to us. It is a day in which we find in Him alone our self-worth. It tells us that He made us and redeemed us. We matter to God.

Distinction between the saved and the lost

The crucial difference between the saved and the lost is this understanding and acceptance of Christ's distinction from them. The saved will experience this distinction in their resting in Him. This is what will get them through the final exodus through end events. This is the essence of the Sabbath. These are the ones who rest in Christ alone and throughout eternity will sing about Him and their experience in the end time (Revelation 14:3; 15:3). It is from this perspective that we need to consider final events, for in Christ they will be a Sabbath rest—a time of deliverance the saints will sing about for all eternity!

Entrance to heaven a gift

Did you do anything to get into this world? Life came to you as a gift. Will you do anything to get into the next world? It is equally a gift, although unlike the first birth, life in the next world can be accepted or rejected. The first thing to realize is that one cannot earn the right to get into the next world anymore than one earned the right to be born in the first place.

It is true that we must be fitted for heaven, but sanctification is a work that only Christ can do. It is a *re*creative work that only a Creator can accomplish. We must remember the distinction between the Creator and creatures, which is the essence of the Sabbath. So often God's people forget and work on as if there were no gift. Through His life, death, and present priestly ministry, Christ has done for the redeemed what they could never do for themselves—He created them and redeemed them. True Sabbath observance means resting in this twofold finished work of Christ.

---

1. *Patriarchs and Prophets*, 36.
2. Ibid., 38.
3. *The Great Controversy*, 438.
4. *Catechism of the Catholic Church* (Liguori, Mo.: Liguori Publications, 1994), 524, 525.
5. Peter Geiermann, *The Convert's Catechism of Catholic Doctrine* (Rockford, Ill.: Tan, 1977), 50.
6. *The Great Controversy*, 438.
7. *The Desire of Ages*, 300.

Chapter 7

Christ
and Babylon

Retired nurse Annie Ortega Kirkwood lives with her husband and sons near Dallas, Texas. She is a Protestant, but she believes the mother of Jesus sends messages to the earth through her. The book *Mary's Message to the World* gives these communications received from 1987 to 1991.[1] Did these messages come from Mary or from a fallen angel who began channeling ideas through Annie? What does "Mary" say?

The alleged Mary promises that she will come to many places with evidences of the supernatural and healings.[2] She claims that she will appear at different places simultaneously.[3] Among her messages about Jesus are these: He "seldom lost his temper,"[4] went to a school located between Nazareth and Egypt at age twelve,[5] was apprenticed to a distant relative at the age of fourteen, and traveled to "learn what He could about other people and the world in general."[6]

"Mary" speaks of experiencing many lifetimes. She claims that she returned to earth in the Middle Ages as a nun and helped establish the Order of the Sisters of Charity. In another lifetime, she supposedly became one of the followers of Saint Francis of Assisi. In another, she and Joseph returned to earth as nuns, but Joseph did not like being a female. Another time, "Mary" returned as a healer in India.[7] "Mary" claims that reincarnation can take place "one at a time, and, at times, two or more at a time."[8] This means that someone can return to earth as two or more distinct people at the same time! Further, "Mary" claims that "the spirit is the essence, the God-part of you,"[9] that heaven and hell are "simply mental states," that man "will evolve into a new species,"[10] and people "will be able to communicate with those who are living in the spirit world."[11]

The book ends with an alleged message from Jesus (chapter 10). According to "Mary," He assures us that "there are no requirements to precede eternal life."[12] "It will be in your mind that the voice of God will guide you."[13] He refers to the book of Revelation. "The seven churches are representative of the major religions."[14] "The 144,000 are representative of the people who belong to the major religions."[15] In connection with Revelation 8:13, Jesus says, "The remainder of the book of Revelation explains the coming events, but you have a better guide in Mother Mary because she has given you her predictions and the times in which these events will occur."[16]

These statements contradict the Bible by claiming that Mary lived on after death, that she and others can be in more than one place at the same time (qualities possessed only by an omnipresent God), that one can communicate with the spirit world, that eternal life is not based upon beliefs but upon the reincarnation, that all religions are equally valid ways to the kingdom. The fact that the alleged Christ calls attention to Mary as a better guide than the inspired book of Revelation calls in question the uniqueness of God's revelation in Scripture.

Ever since Satan called God's statement "you shall surely die" into question in Eden (Genesis 3:1-4), he has continued to deceive humankind by statements that are opposed to Scripture. Just as he uses individuals, such as Annie Kirkwood, so he has used nations and churches to teach doctrines contrary to Scripture. Jesus said, "In vain they do worship me, teaching for doctrines the commandments of men" (Matthew 15:9, KJV). Satan is the author of confusion through contradicting what God has said.

First space venture

The first space venture took place soon after the Flood. Those opposed to God built the tower of Babel. *Babel* means "confusion," according to Genesis 11:9, based on the Hebrew verb *balal*, which means "to confuse."[17] We need to consider what was going on in that venture. It has a direct bearing on end-time events.

God says, "The dwellers on the plain of Shinar disbelieved God's covenant that he would not again bring a flood upon the earth. Many of them denied the existence of God, and attributed the flood to the operation of natural causes. Others believed in a supreme being, and that it was he who had destroyed the antediluvian world; and their hearts, like that of Cain, rose up in rebellion against him. One object before them in the erection of the tower of Babel was to secure their own safety in case of another deluge. By carrying the structure to a much greater height than was reached by the waters of the flood, they thought to place themselves beyond all possibility of danger. And as they would be able to ascend to the region of the clouds, they hoped to ascertain the cause of the flood. The whole undertaking was designed to exalt still further the pride of its projectors, and to turn the minds of future generations away from God, and lead them into idolatry."[18]

The Tower of Babel was humankind's attempt to save itself (Genesis 11:1-9). The builders thought they would not need an ark to save them if another flood came. They would build above the flood line. "We don't need You, God!" The project was a false plan of salvation for the next deluge. They did not heed the lesson of Noah's ark, that God alone can supply salvation (Genesis 6:14-22). More than that, they did not heed His promise never to send another flood (Genesis 9:15). Their building was in vain.

Moreover, God said the people should disperse throughout the world (verses 1, 2). By contrast, the city and tower "were designed to prevent the people from scattering abroad in colonies. . . . These Babel builders determined to keep their community united in one body, and to found a monarchy that should eventually embrace the whole earth. Thus their city would become the metropolis of a universal empire; its glory would command the admiration and homage of the world and render the founders illustrious."[19]

These Babel builders practiced a false religion. They corrupted offerings established by Christ with Adam after his fall. God says, "They had no faith in the Redeemer to come, and they sacrificed to gods of their own choosing, instead of the God of Heaven. Their superstition led them to great extravagances. They taught the people that the more valuable their offerings, the greater would be the pleasure of their gods, and consequently the greater the prosperity and riches of their nation. Hence, human beings were often sacrificed to these senseless idols. Many of the laws which governed these nations were cruel in the extreme. They were made by men whose hearts were not softened by divine grace, and while the most debasing crimes were passed over lightly, a small offense would be visited by the most cruel punishment."[20]

We could summarize these three quotations as follows. The tower builders:

• Disbelieved God's word.
• Rejected His method of salvation.
• Substituted a works system of sacrifices to gods.
• Were involved in uniting the world under them.
• Passed cruel laws.

We will need to return to this list when we consider modern Babylon. But first a word about ancient Babylon.

Ancient Babylon—a nation

Ancient Babylon took Judah into captivity at the time of Daniel. It was King Nebuchadnezzar who erected the image on the Plain of Dura. God's version of the king's dream limited the gold to the head of the image (Daniel 2:32-45). Babylon would be overcome by Medo-Persia and it by Greece and it by Rome and it by the separated kingdoms and they by God's eternal kingdom. Nebuchadnezzar, like the tower builders, rejected this forecast of history and so built the whole image of gold, as if Babylon was the eternal kingdom (Daniel 3:1). This image was man-made, in contrast to the image Nebuchadnezzar saw in his dream. This was a counterfeit kingdom in place of God's eternal kingdom, because Nebuchadnezzar refused to heed the word of God about the image in his dream. But he didn't stop there. He went on to declare a decree, that all should fall down and worship this image (verses 2-5). Here was counterfeit worship, with a death decree to enforce it (verses 3:6). What a striking resemblance to the Babel builders!

Whereas Babel's tower stood more than three hundred feet high, the image of gold arose to ninety feet (verse 1). Both projects glorified the rulers in defiance of God and His word.

Three Hebrew worthies dwelt in Babylon. They heard the command "Bow or burn!" They refused to bow. They stood tall while all others cowered and worshiped a false image. The king was furious (verse 13) and ordered the furnace to be heated seven times hotter, then gave the command to bow once more (verses 13-20). These three knew their God. He alone was worthy of their worship. They would have nothing to do with counterfeit worship. They would rather die than turn from their God (verses 17, 18). What would you do if you looked at that blazing furnace? Would you bow or stand tall?

You know the story so well. They were thrown into the furnace. But they did not burn. How do you think they felt? "Wow, we are the first men in history to survive a fiery furnace! We are ready for the *Guinness Book of World Records.*" No, a thousand times no! They stood in awe. It dawned on them that they were not alone. "God is in here with us. Praise God from whom all blessings flow! Hallelujah! What a Saviour!" For four men were seen walking about in the furnace that day. Onlookers exclaimed, They are "unbound and unharmed, and the fourth looks like a son of the gods" (verse 25).

Babylon—the church

While in Babylon, Daniel dreamed about four beasts and a little horn that came out of the ten horns of the fourth beast (Daniel 7). This little horn began to exert itself after three of the ten horns were uprooted (verses 8, 20, 24). Here is papal Rome rising out of pagan Rome. What does this little horn do? Does it have a program similar to the Babel builders'? Consider the following. It is boastful (verses 8, 11, 20), wages war against God's saints (verses 21, 25), speaks against God (verse

25), and tries to change the time and the law (verse 25).

It is important to note that the little horn is also called "the beast" and that it will be cast into a "blazing fire" (verse 11). The nation Babylon had a fiery furnace for God's people, and Babylon as a church has burned great numbers of martyrs at the stake; but God has the last word—a blazing fire for the beast. The book of Revelation mentions this fire. "I saw the beast and the kings of the earth and their armies gathered together to make war against the rider on the horse and his army. But the beast was captured, and with him the false prophet who had performed the miraculous signs on his behalf. With these signs he had deluded those who had received the mark of the beast and worshiped his image. The two of them were thrown alive into the fiery lake of burning sulfur" (Revelation 19:19, 20).

In the book of Revelation, Babylon and the New Jerusalem are identified with the two sides in the great controversy, Satan's and Christ's. In the end time, these two groups are represented by the beast and the group of 144,000 sealed saints. Others join with the beast whom we consider in the next section. The beast will have an image "set up" in its honor (Revelation 13:14, compare verse 3). The image in the nation of Babylon was to honor the king and to defy God. The coming image to the beast will honor the beast and defy God. The whole world will be made to worship this beast (verse 12). Those, like the Hebrew worthies, who refuse to worship the counterfeit will have a death decree enacted against them (verse 15). Everyone on planet Earth will bow to worship the beast (verses 3, 4), except God's end-time saints. Now, Babylon is more than a nation. It is a global force; it fulfills the desire of the Babel builders. It was precisely to delay this plan that Christ confused the languages at Babel so that the designs of the builders to make a global union against God could be interrupted. The good news is this. Although there will be martyrs before probation's close (Revelation 20:4), none of God's people will die from the death decree, as it comes after the close of probation.[21]

The image of Nebuchadnezzar was a counterfeit for the image God gave him in his dream. Likewise, the coming Sunday laws are a counterfeit for the Sabbath given to humankind by Christ. The issue is, whom will you worship? In Revelation 13 and 14, worship is mentioned eight times. The test over worship in the nation of Babylon has escalated to a global test in spiritual Babylon. The antitype is informed by the type. There is coming a fiery furnace for God's people. Daniel speaks about it. "At that time Michael, the great prince who protects your people, will arise. There will be a time of distress such as has not happened from the beginning of nations until then. But at that time your people—everyone whose name is found written in the book—will be delivered" (Daniel 12:1).

Christ will stand in the midst of the fiery furnace with us, as He did with the three Hebrew worthies. He promised, "I am with you always, to the very end of the age" (Matthew 28:20). He does not bail out before we do. He stays with us to take us through. He has guaranteed, "Never will I leave you; never will I forsake you" (Hebrews 13:5). He will keep us (Jude 24) and deliver us out of the time of trouble, just as He did for the three Hebrews.

So the papacy has the same five problems of the Babel builders. It opposes God's Word; has its own method of salvation, through its own works; and will have the world unite under it and pass a death decree against all who oppose it.

Mary, not Christ, is exalted by the papacy. In the book *The Glories of Mary*, Cardinal and Saint Alphonsus de Liguori says, "Sinners receive pardon by . . . Mary alone. He falls and is lost who has not recourse to Mary. Mary is called . . . the gate of Heaven because no one can enter that blessed kingdom without passing through her."[22] No wonder people flock to apparitions of Mary around the world! Vatican II (1963–1965) documents and the latest Catechism (1994) give official insight into the elevation of Mary.

Babylon and the churches

The papacy is the woman riding the beast in Revelation 17. Dave Hunt's book, *A Woman Rides the Beast*, gives an excellent insight into the end-time Catholic church.[23] Revelation 17 presents the woman (or church, compare Jeremiah

6:2) who is "drunk with the blood of the saints" (Revelation 17:6). On her forehead is a title, "MYSTERY BABYLON THE GREAT THE MOTHER OF PROSTITUTES AND THE ABOMINATIONS OF THE EARTH" (verse 5). The woman (papacy) has daughters (Protestant churches); she has led them astray. They keep her Sunday and will worship the papacy in the end time.

The second angel's message awaits Babylon's complete fulfillment when "all nations drink the maddening wine of her adulteries" (Revelation 14:8). Before that time, God sends His final invitation, "Come out of her, my people (Revelation 18:4). Multitudes today, in all churches, remain unaware of the Sabbath issue. They will learn the importance of the Sabbath for the first time when they hear the final invitation. These people already belong to Christ. They love Him and worship Him with all their hearts.

Recently, I attended an International Congress on the Family co-sponsored by Focus on the Family and the American Association of Christian Counselors that convened in Denver, Colorado, July 5 to 8, 1995. Some three thousand Christians gathered from different denominations. We worshiped together each day, and oh, how these Christians manifested their love for Christ! They worshiped Him with joy and freedom. I was greatly blessed! Jesus said, "Other sheep I have, which are not of this fold" (John 10:16, KJV). These are His people today. The amazing Promise Keepers movement, in which men get together and make commitments is another example of His people. This year, sixty-two thousand men met in Atlanta, Georgia; and sixty-four thousand in Seattle, Washington. Willow Creek Christians in Chicago reach out to the unchurched and have an impact across America. Many of these beautiful Christians will one day stand up in the final test on the modern Plain of Dura and not bow to the final image to the beast. They will stand firm with us, and Christ will stand with us all. For all have come out of Babylon, renounced human ideas and methods, and learned to trust in Christ alone.

This day is coming soon!

1. Annie Kirkwood, *Mary's Message to the World* (New York: Putnam's Sons, 1991).

2. Ibid., 41-43.

3. Ibid., 44.

4. Ibid., 65.

5. Ibid., 66.

6. Ibid., 67.

7. Ibid., 82-85.

8. Ibid., 193.

9. Ibid., 193.

10. Ibid., 243.

11. Ibid., 247.

12. Ibid., 264.

13. Ibid., 266.

14. Ibid., 268.

15. Ibid., 271.

16. Ibid., 275.

17. *Seventh-day Adventist Bible Dictionary*, revised edition (Hagerstown, Md.: Review and Herald, 1979), 108.

18. Ellen G. White, *Christian Education*, 208.

19. *Patriarchs and Prophets*, 119.

20. Ellen G. White, "The Law of Moses," *Signs of the Times*, 17 May 1880, 9.

21. *The Great Controversy*, 631.

22. Dave Hunt, *A Woman Rides the Beast* (Eugene, Ore.: Harvest House, 1994), quoted on 439.

23. See ibid., passim.

Chapter 8

Christ
and a Counterfeit Trinity

In the previous chapter, we considered Christ and Babylon. Jesus said, "I am the truth" (John 14:6). Also, "anyone who has seen me has seen the Father" (verse 9). So the Father is the truth, and the Holy Spirit is called the "Spirit of truth" (John 15:26). The Trinity of God are true, and they originate and disseminate truth. By contrast, Satan is called the father of lies (John 8:44). He has a counterfeit trinity that promotes falsehood. In this chapter, we will take a further look at Babylon and note its contrast with Christ.

The Roman Catholic Church

While I taught in the Seventh-day Adventist Theological Seminary (Far East) in Manila, we had a class each summer that studied the sixteen documents of Vatican II (1963–1965). This council, perhaps more than any other event, projects to Protestants the supposed change in Catholic thinking. Yet as one studies the facts, the changes remain only superficial, such as saying the Mass in the native language of the country rather than in Latin. It is still the Mass, in which the priest believes he creates Christ from the elements of bread and wine (transubstantiation) and then crucifies Him afresh. This flies in the face of a finished work of Christ, once for all, as taught in the book of Hebrews (Hebrews 9:25, 26).

It is true that this is the first of the twenty-one ecumenical councils that addresses other churches and religions, but the

Catholic Church continues to consider itself the center of God's activity for the world's salvation. Throughout the documents, the church claims to be the extension of Christ's incarnation. God communicates to Christians through the church, and Christians get help from God through the Catholic Church. "For it is through Christ's Catholic Church alone, which is the all-embracing means of salvation, that the fullness of the means of salvation can be obtained."[1]

On January 25, 1985, Pope John Paul II convoked an extraordinary assembly of the Synod of Bishops for the twentieth anniversary of the close of Vatican Council II. The Synod fathers expressed the need for a Catholic Catechism to continue the work begun at Vatican II. So the pope commissioned twelve cardinals and bishops, under Cardinal Joseph Ratzinger, to prepare the Catechism, a work that took six years. The *Catechism of the Catholic Church* was published in 1994 as "a statement of the Church's faith and of Catholic doctrine."[2]

In this catechism, we find the church's teaching that Christ "extends his reign over all things" through the church.[3] Moreover, "Christ and his Church . . . together make up the 'whole Christ,'" so that they can even say, "We have become Christ."[4] "It is in the Church that 'the fullness of the means of salvation' has been deposited. It is in her that 'by the grace of God we acquire holiness.'"[5] Therefore, "to reunite all his children, scattered and led astray by sin, the Father willed to call the whole of humanity together into his Son's Church. The Church is the place where humanity must rediscover its unity and salvation. The Church is 'the world reconciled.' . . . She is prefigured by Noah's ark, which alone saved from the flood."[6]

The Roman Catholic Church puts itself in the place of Christ. Daniel saw this anti-Christ power. "It set itself up to be as great as the Prince of the host [Christ]; it took away the daily sacrifice from him, and the place of his sanctuary was brought low" (Daniel 8:11). It set up its own priestly ministry on earth to take the place of Christ's high-priestly ministry in heaven.

The counterfeit Trinity

Revelation 13 introduces a counterfeit trinity.[7] This chapter begins the eschatological, or last-day events, section of Revelation. Chapter 12 is an important context. In just seventeen verses, it gives an overview of the great controversy between Christ and Satan. Satan is represented by the dragon (verse 9). Twice the chapter mentions his departure from heaven. Verse 4 says, "His tail swept a third of the stars out of the sky and flung them to the earth." Thus Satan caused the ejection of angels from heaven. Verses 7 and 8 show that Michael (Christ) won the battle against Satan and his angels. Then the focus moves to Satan's final expulsion from heaven, in verses 9 to 13, when he led the whole world astray (verse 9), hence, during human history. We noted in chapter 1 that this took place at Calvary (see verses 9-12).

Of all final events, Calvary is the most important one. Those who gaze at Calvary will not fear final events to come. To fear final events is to forget *that* final event. Satan was defeated at the cross. These verses in Revelation 12 are approximately the central ones in the book of Revelation. It is as if the historical section of Revelation climaxes at the cross, and the eschatological section foretelling end events begins with the Calvary final event.

This brings good news to God's people. Calvary towers above end-time events as the decisive and determining victory qualifying them all. Satan cannot win in the end time because he has already lost the war, and it is only a matter of time till this is seen in stark clarity. This is the context for our study of the counterfeit trinity. They have no future. They are doomed by Christ's completed work at Calvary.

Counterfeit Father and Son

In Revelation 13:1, John sees the dragon Satan standing on the shore of the sea while a sea beast arises out of the waters (representing a populated area; Revelation 17:15). "He had ten horns and seven heads." In Revelation 12:3, the red dragon has "seven heads and ten horns." So these are look-alikes. They both have seven heads and ten horns. I believe the dragon is a counterfeit for God the Father and the sea beast is a counterfeit for Christ. We have already noted above that the Catholic Church identifies itself as Christ on earth, and the sea beast is Catholicism. Jesus said, "Anyone who has seen me has seen the Father" (John 14:9). They are look-alikes.

Then "the dragon gave the beast his power and his throne and great authority" (Revelation 13:2). Jesus said, "All authority in heaven and on earth has been given to me" (Matthew 28:18). He further said that authority came from His Father (John 10:18). So just as the Father gives authority to Christ, Satan gives authority to the papacy.

Furthermore, the papacy had a deadly wound and later was restored (Revelation 13:3), just as Christ died and was resurrected. The papacy ministers for forty-two prophetic months (verse 5), just as Christ ministered for forty-two literal months. Clearly, there are several parallels between Satan and the papacy on one side and the Father and Christ on the other.

The counterfeit Holy Spirit

Then John saw "another beast, coming out of the earth" (Revelation 13:11). The earth is the opposite of waters. Whereas waters represent peoples (Revelation 17:15), the earth represents a comparatively unpopulated area. I have just returned from Beijing, China. Soon after the Tower of Babel dispersion of peoples to the whole world (Genesis 11:8), people came to the territory of mainland China. The Chinese have a long history, and today, comprise one-fifth of the world population. But the population of the Americas was quite low before the Pilgrims landed.

To these shores, the Pilgrims fled from Catholic oppression in the Old World (Revelation 12:16). Here they found a safe haven (note that the wilderness in Europe functioned in the same way previously; Revelation 12:6, 14). Here the separation of church and state became constitutional. Here God began His end-time church which now engulfs the world. God kept this continent for the end time, to protect the persecuted pilgrims and to establish His church. He knew that this would be the best center from which to reach the world. As the strategic geographical area of Palestine was chosen by God to reach the world in bygone days, so He has used America to form His advent movement to reach the world in the end time.

The time of Revelation 13:11-18

What time is John primarily focusing on in Revelation 13? To answer this, we need to compare the crowns in this chapter with those in chapter 12. In chapter 12, the crowns are on the seven heads (verse 3). In chapter 13, the crowns are on the ten horns (verse 1). Both the dragon (Satan) and the sea beast (papacy) have seven heads and ten horns. The only difference between them is the placement of the crowns. Is there any significance in this difference? I believe there is. We need to let Scripture interpret itself. Revelation 17 contains the answer. Here the woman (representing the papacy, apostate Protestantism, and spiritualism) is seated on a beast (the state) which has seven heads and ten horns (verse 3).

"This calls for a mind with wisdom. The seven heads are seven hills on which the woman sits [Rome]. They are also seven kings. Five have fallen, one is, the other has not yet come; but when he does come, he must remain for a little while" (verses 9, 10). What does this information mean, in the context of a woman riding on a beast or a church riding the state? All the heads are kings in a similar union. The five that are fallen may include Egypt, Assyria, Babylon, Medo-Persia, and Greece (compare the image of Daniel 2). The "one is" refers to pagan Rome, and the one to come is papal Rome, the little horn of Daniel 7 and the sea beast of Revelation 13.

What about the ten horns? "The ten horns you saw are ten kings who have not yet received a kingdom, but who for one hour will receive authority as kings along with the beast" (Revelation 17:12). This is still future from our time. It coincides with Revelation 13:3, 4, where the whole world worships the dragon and the papacy. This is reinforced by Revelation 17:13, 14: "They have one purpose and will give their power and authority to the beast. They will make war against the Lamb, but the Lamb will overcome them."

So the seven heads are kings that come successively to power, whereas the ten horns are kings that reign together for one short hour with the beast, in their future tenuous union, between the time of the institution of Sunday laws and the beginning of Armageddon. Revelation 12 covers the entire overview of the great controversy but primarily focuses on when the seven heads are reigning. Revelation 13 covers the period from the rise of the papacy to the death decree but primarily focuses on the end time.

The earth beast

The earth beast is described as "another beast" (Revelation 13:11) with reference to the sea beast (verse 1). In the Greek, there are two words for "another" (*allos*, same or *heteros*, different). This beast is the same as the papacy. The word for "beast" is *therion*, meaning "wild beast." So the earth beast, America, is immediately portrayed as a wild beast. This beast speaks as a dragon but looks like a lamb. Some see this as predicting America's lamblike beginning and dragonlike end. But it remains a wild beast from the beginning. The lamblike exterior covers the dragonlike agenda, particularly in the end time. America fulfills this description today. The Christian Coalition, for example, seems lamblike, but its agenda may well lead to the expected Sunday law.

Image to the beast

Values are important. I heard Dr. William Bennett in Denver, Colorado, on July 5, 1995. He gave the keynote address at the International Convention on the Family. He said that *The Book of Virtues* he edited with commentary had already sold 2.2 million copies.[8] Values, or virtues, are being talked about today. The problem with the American government in the end time is its lamblike interest in virtues, its agenda to enforce its view of morality on all. This will be its dragonlike, or satanic quality, for it will pass a Sunday law with an eventual death decree to enforce it (Revelation 13:15).

The image of the beast is not the Sunday law. The image looks like what it images. The beast (papacy) is a union of church and state. It is in the joining of church and state that America will form an image to the beast. One result of that image will be a Sunday law and a death decree. I believe that the image to the beast may well be forming now, as the Christian Coalition impacts government as never before.

But there is more in Revelation 13. Of America it says, "He exercised all the authority of the first beast on his behalf, and made the earth and its inhabitants worship the first beast" (verse 12). Could this have been accomplished while there were two superpowers? No. The stage is now set for this fulfillment. How will a mostly non-Christian world be interested in worshiping the papacy, which means, in part, obeying an international Sunday law? We need to consider this in context.

The Lamb is mentioned twenty-eight times in Revelation. Only once does it refer to something other than Christ (Revelation 13:11). America is like the Lamb, just as the Holy Spirit is like Christ. Jesus said the Holy Spirit "will bring glory to me" (John 16:14). The Holy Spirit is self-effacing. He brings Christ to dwell with all humankind (John 14:15-18). Those within whom the Holy Spirit dwells are Christians, not Spiritans. The Holy Spirit does not add to the plan of salvation, to get us to heaven. The journey to heaven is not like a two-stage rocket, with Christ's life, death, and resurrection getting us into space and the Holy Spirit coming to take us the rest of the journey. Christ said He is the way to the Father (verse 6).

Just as the Holy Spirit ministers to bring glory to Christ, so America will minister in the end time to bring glory to the papacy. America, in its role as a counterfeit Holy Spirit, will make the inhabitants of the world worship the papacy (Revelation 13:12).

What causes the world to unite?

From a human perspective, a mostly non-Christian world doesn't seem a likely candidate to keep a so-called "Christian" Sunday law. Will the world be brought to its knees through financial collapse, through devastating natural disasters, or through fear of a nuclear holocaust or all of the above? Will common survival be the motive to try anything to escape the inevitable? Whatever it is, we do know that Satan will work to unite the world, just as he tried to do when the tower of Babel was built. But this time, he will succeed. The counterfeit Trinity will play its part.

The beast which represents America will be given power to perform "great and miraculous signs, even causing fire to come down from heaven. . . . Because of the signs he was given power to do on behalf of the first beast [the papacy], he deceived the inhabitants of the earth" (Revelation 13:13, 14). Revelation 16:14 speaks of "spirits of demons performing miraculous signs, and they go out to the kings of the whole world, to gather them for the battle on the great day of God Almighty." Satan appealed to the senses in the Garden of Eden. Eve saw that the fruit was beneficial, and she ate it (Genesis 3:6). "Seeing is believing" constituted Satan's trump card in Eden, and it will be again in the end time on a global scale.

One sign is specified—"fire from heaven." This could have two meanings. Just as the Holy Spirit came in tongues of fire at Pentecost (Acts 2:3), so the charismatic movement, which has done so much to unite Christian churches, will sweep over the world to unite it under Satan. It is a counterfeit Pentecost. Did not God say, "Satan determines to unite them in one body and thus strengthen his cause by sweeping all into the ranks of spiritualism"?[9] The other possible significance of this sign is that it represents a repetition of the Mt. Carmel test to prove who is God (1 Kings 18:16-40).

Satan comes as Christ

Besides the counterfeit Trinity, with Satan as the counterfeit Father behind the scenes, we come now to his manifestation as Christ. This is "the crowning act in the great drama of deception." Christians have longed for the coming of Christ. "Now the great deceiver will make it appear that Christ has come. In different parts of the earth, Satan will manifest himself among men as a majestic being of dazzling brightness, resembling the description of the Son of God given by John in Revelation. Revelation 1:13-15. The glory that surrounds him is unsurpassed by anything that mortal eyes have yet beheld. The shout of triumph rings out upon the air: 'Christ has come!

Christ has come!' The people prostrate themselves in adoration before him, while he lifts up his hands and pronounces a blessing upon them, as Christ blessed His disciples when He was upon the earth. His voice is soft and subdued, yet full of melody. In gentle, compassionate tones he presents some of the same gracious, heavenly truths which the Saviour uttered; he heals the diseases of the people, and then, in his assumed character of Christ, he claims to have changed the Sabbath to Sunday, and commands all to hallow the day which he has blessed."[10]

This is why the worried world will obey. For Satan "will cause fire to come down from heaven in the sight of men, to prove that he is God."[11] How despicable the deceiver and deception! He parades as the great liberator, when Christ has already soundly defeated Him at the cross.

---

1. *The Documents of Vatican II* (London: Chapman, 1966), 346.
2. *Catechism of the Catholic Church* (Liguori, Mo.: Liguori, 1994), 5.
3. Ibid., 209.
4. Ibid., 210.
5. Ibid., 218.
6. Ibid., 224.
7. For ideas in this section, see Jon Paulien, *What the Bible Says About the End Time* (Hagerstown, Md.: Review and Herald, 1994), 109-111.
8. William J. Bennett, *The Book of Virtues* (New York: Simon & Schuster, 1993).
9. *The Great Controversy*, 588.
10. Ibid., 624.
11. Ellen G. White, *Medical Ministry*, 88.

Chapter 9

Christ
and His Seal

Down in the basement of a tall building in Hong Kong, Bibles stood stashed away on shelves. We descended to get our consignment for a special mission to mainland China. We tucked sixty Bibles in with our clothes in three cases. I thought of Brother Andrew (author of the book *God's Smuggler*), who has smuggled Bibles across many dangerous barriers for forty years. I had no idea that a few weeks later we would meet in Denver, Colorado.

Two others planned to cross the border with me: my wife, Leona, and my former student, Daniel Jiao, who works in the East Asia Association, producing radio programs in Mandarin for the Chinese people.

On the morrow, we moved slowly toward the custom officers. How they scrutinized the passports! The wait seemed endless. Friends instructed us what to do after the passport check—just walk through customs as if we knew where we were going. My wife and I did this. No one stopped us, and the Bibles crossed the border without any problem. What a relief. "Thank You, Lord!" But Daniel was delayed. We wondered why. He had my wife's bigger case, and she had his smaller one. "What if they open it and find it is not his and discover the Bibles too?" We waited anxiously, praying.

Finally, we saw him come through customs and tried to read his face. When he drew nearer, he whispered, "It's OK. They saw all the visas in my passport and wondered if I was a dissi-

81

dent. They checked my name against a long list." We were relieved. All sixty Bibles were safe. And what joy we had that night in Beijing as we handed the Bibles over to two people who would distribute them to others.

A few weeks later, I talked to Brother Andrew in Denver, Colorado. I wondered about 1997, when mainland China takes over Hong Kong. I asked him, "Will we still be able to get Bibles in then?"

"No one knows," he replied. This is the same answer others had given. "The people are responding to the gospel in China in greater numbers than anywhere else in the world." Brother Andrew knew from his contacts. What a tragedy that the vast majority do not even have a Bible. What a challenge to get Bibles into China while the door remains open!

God's Word

"None but those who have fortified the mind with the truths of the Bible will stand through the last great conflict."[1] What a sobering statement! I like to read it in the positive. "All those who have fortified their minds with the truths of the Bible will stand in the last great conflict." This is one reason why all efforts are being made to get Bibles to the Chinese. What a blessing to have a Bible! The Bibles in China are cherished, loved, used. How about your Bible?

Christ's saints commune with Christ through His Word. Recently, in Japan, I visited an Adventist brother ninety-seven years old. I picked up his Bible and leafed through it. He had written notes in it from cover to cover. He prizes his Bible. How about us? Do we spend more time with the Bible than with TV, videos, or the newspaper? It is time to get into *the Book*. "When the testing time shall come, those who have made God's word their rule of life will be revealed."[2] It will be too late to begin Bible study then.

The shaking in God's remnant church

What will happen when the testing time arrives, when Sunday laws are passed? "When the law of God is made void the church will be sifted by fiery trials, and a larger proportion than we now anticipate, will give heed to seducing spirits and doctrines of devils."[3] Think of this in view of Revelation 16:12-16. There it speaks of these spirits of devils who go to the whole world to gather them to Satan's side for the battle of Armageddon. Could it be that even Adventists will be taken in? After all, they know which is the right day to keep. They know the seventh day is Saturday and not Sunday. But much more is involved. It is more than mathematics. It is not just the Sabbath but a relationship with the Lord of the Sabbath that makes the crucial difference. This is why Sunday keepers who have a relationship with Christ now are safe. It is only a matter of time till they learn of the Sabbath and change. I would rather be a Sunday keeper who loves Christ than an Adventist who goes to church on the Sabbath but doesn't know Christ. Wouldn't you?

How many will leave our church? "Soon God's people will be tested by fiery trials, and the great proportion of those who now appear to be genuine and true will prove to be base metal."[4] In fact, "the church may appear as about to fall, but it does not fall. It remains, while the sinners in Zion will be sifted out—the chaff separated from the precious wheat. This is a terrible ordeal, but nevertheless it must take place."[5] What a heart-rending experience this will be! We will need to be sealed to endure.

Jesus spoke of this day. Candidates for the sealing will be betrayed by their own family as Jesus was by Judas. They will be willing to die for Christ and His truth. Jesus said, "Then you will be handed over to be persecuted and put to death, and you will be hated by all nations because of me. At that time many will turn away from the faith and will betray and hate each other" (Matthew 24:9, 10). "Brother will betray brother to death, and a father his child. Children will rebel against their parents and have them put to death. All men will hate you because of me, but he who stands firm to the end will be saved" (Mark 13:12, 13). A special group of God's people are mentioned in the millennium—those who were martyred in the end time. They will rule with Christ on thrones for a thousand years (Revelation 20:4).

The most important period in last-day events

What do you suppose is the most important period of last-day events? Is it between the Sunday law and the close of probation? Is it after the close of probation? Is it the battle of Armageddon? Is it the time just before the second advent? No, none of these. The most important period is from today till the latter rain. For preparation to receive the latter rain is the only way to experience all end-time events and be saved.

Think of it. The Jews expected Christ to come. But when He came, He didn't come according to their expectations. They looked for His coming in glory—as a conquering Messiah to liberate them from the hated Romans. They totally overlooked His quiet coming as a babe. So it is today. We may be looking for His coming in glory and overlook His quiet advent through the Holy Spirit. We know that the Holy Spirit, since Pentecost, always brings Christ to humankind. We must be ready for this advent that precedes the second coming of Christ.

The most important thing for Seventh-day Adventists is to be ready for the second advent of the Holy Spirit, the second Pentecost, the outpouring of the latter rain. In fact, if we are ready for the second advent of the Holy Spirit, then we will be ready for the second coming of Christ. Conversely, if we are not ready for the second coming of the Holy Spirit, we will not be ready for the second coming of Christ. This is because the second coming of the Holy Spirit is the sealing Holy Spirit, who comes to take us through final events on planet Earth.

The work of sealing

Sealing is the only way through final events for Christ's saints. It is their passport. Without it, they cannot go through and be saved. What is the sealing? God says, it is "a settling into the truth, both intellectually and spiritually, so they cannot be moved."[6] This is why knowing the truth is not enough. The heart is a vital part of the sealing. When does this come? Christ's people must be sealed before the Sunday-law test, or they would be moved. The preparation must precede the Sunday laws. This means they must be getting ready now. It means they must now be settling into the truth, both intellectually and spiritually. It is only after a process in which the Holy Spirit is leading them into a deeper relationship with Christ and a greater commitment to His truth that they stand ready for sealing.

The sealing is the final endorsement of the Holy Spirit. It will have a profound effect upon Christ's followers. Have you ever put a fence post into the ground? You remember how the concrete mix is pliable when wet, and you can easily change the position of the post. But after a few hours, the concrete has hardened, and the post is immovable. Now is the final time for Christ's saints to get their roots into Scripture; to really know Christ, whom to know is life eternal (John 17:3); to be so settled into truth, intellectually (know it) and spiritually (love it), that they remain immovable, sealed. The post has to get into the concrete to become immovable. The saints have to get into Scripture, and into an ever-deepening relationship with Christ, to be sealed.

Besides wonderful fellowship with my Adventist brothers and sisters, I enjoy mingling with evangelicals from various churches. So many inspire me with their love for Christ, and they need to know about our church. At one meeting, Dr. Les Parott spoke of a three-day silence retreat. That got my attention. One usually goes to a retreat to listen to speakers. "The first day at the silence retreat nearly drives you batty," he said. "You go to eat with others at mealtime but do not talk. You avoid eye contact." Can you imagine how hard it would be? "Then you go back to your room to read the Gospel of John. The first day is the hardest. You pore over John's Gospel and plead for understanding. By the second day, you are ready to hear the voice of God through Scripture. By the third day, ideas from the text come to you as God's Spirit leads." What a great idea!

At another meeting, some Christians spoke of fasting and praying till they could discern God's will through Scripture. Jesus said, "Blessed are those who hunger and thirst for righteousness, for they will be filled" (Matthew 5:6). These are candidates for the sealing, even though they keep Sunday and know nothing about the Sabbath yet. Oh, that I may hunger after the Word as they do!

The thief in the night for Adventists

When is the thief-in-the-night experience for Seventh-day Adventists? After all, many of us have last-day-events charts memorized. We know that the Sunday law launches the early time of trouble that is over at the close of probation, which begins the great time of trouble. Jacob's trouble is a part of the second period, beginning at the death decree and going to the sixth plague. Then comes Armageddon and the second advent. How could the second advent ever be a surprise to Adventists who know the chart?

The fact is this: the thief-in-the-night experience is the very next event for Adventists. There is no event to precede it. To be unprepared for the sealing latter rain is the thief in the night for Adventists. It is after this sealing latter rain comes that the recipients will be filled with power to give the last invitation. Then will go forth the call "Come out of her, my people" (Revelation 18:4). Then "large numbers will be admitted who in these last days hear the truth for the first time."[7]

"That's not fair," shouts some observant thinker. "Why do they still have a chance to be sealed, when a great majority of Adventists have lost theirs?"

"It's really simple," comes the reply. "They had to get ready long before, just like Adventists. The only difference is, they did not know about the Sabbath. It takes time to grow into a relationship with Christ. It takes less time to assent to new truth."

Christ's security in the sealing

Candidates for the sealing are willing to die for Christ. There will be some martyrs in the end time. But there is another side to this. The sealing is mentioned in Revelation in connection with the 144,000 (Revelation 7:1-4) These are those who will live through final events and be translated (Revelation 14:1-4). Ellen White says, "The sealing is a pledge from God of perfect security to His chosen ones (Ex 31:13-17). Sealing indicates you are God's chosen. He has appropriated you to Himself. As the sealed of God we are Christ's purchased possession, and no one shall pluck us out of His hands."[8]

In mercy, Christ waits

Revelation 7 tells us that four angels hold back winds of strife that wait to be unleashed upon the earth (verses 1-4).

In the August 1, 1849, edition of *Present Truth*, Ellen White penned these words. "The Spirit fell upon me, and I was taken off in vision. I saw four angels who had a work to do on the earth, and were on their way to accomplish it. Jesus was clothed with Priestly garments. He gazed in pity on the remnant, then raised his hands upward, and with a voice of deep pity cried, 'My Blood, Father, My Blood, My Blood, My Blood.' Then I saw an exceeding bright light come from God, who sat upon the great white throne, and was shed all about Jesus. Then I saw an angel with a commission from Jesus, swiftly flying to the four angels who had a work to do on the earth, and waving something up and down in his hand, and crying with a loud voice, "Hold! Hold! Hold! Hold! until the servants of God are sealed in their foreheads."[9] That was 147 years ago! But Christ will not wait much longer. Evidence abounds on every side that He is coming soon. The latter rain is almost upon us. God's power is coming to take us through. It is time to get into the modern ark to go through the final storm. It is time to find in Christ our only refuge.

"In a little while every one who is a child of God will have His seal placed upon him. O, that it may be placed upon our foreheads! Who can endure the thought of being passed by when the angel goes forth to seal the servants of God in their foreheads?"[10]

Only two groups in the end time

The Sabbath is "a sign" between Christ and His followers (Ezekiel 20:12). At the time of the Sunday law, it will become a sign of loyalty for all Christians. The loyal will be sealed. Sunday is not the mark of the beast until the Sunday laws (compare Revelation 13:16). Great numbers of Sunday keepers will one day awaken as from a dream and gladly stand with Sabbath keepers.

Every human will submit in the end to Christ or to Satan. They will worship Christ (Revelation 14:6, 7) or Satan (Revelation 13:4). They will choose Sunday or the Sabbath. "While one class, by accepting the sign of submission to earthly powers, receive the mark of the beast, the other choosing the token of allegiance to divine authority, receive the seal of God."[11]

1. *The Great Controversy*, 593, 594.
2. Ibid., 602.
3. Ellen G. White, *Selected Messages*, 2:368.
4. Ellen G. White, *Testimonies for the Church*, 5:136.
5. *Selected Messages*, 2:380.
6. Ellen G. White, *Last Day Events*, 219.
7. Ibid., 182.
8. Ellen G. White, "Heaven's Judgments on the Wicked; God's People Sealed," *Manuscript Releases*, 15:225.
9. Ellen G. White, "Dear Brethren and Sisters," *The Present Truth*, 1 August 1849.
10. Ellen G. White Comments, *SDA Bible Commentary*, 7:969, 970.
11. *The Great Controversy*, 605.

Chapter 10

Christ
in the Early Time of Trouble

Alexander studied in the Zhanjiang Teacher's College in China. He became a Seventh-day Adventist recently. During his first term, he made several visits to his head teacher to ask permission to skip Sabbath classes. The teacher flatly refused but seemed to sympathize with him. When the second term began, Alexander decided to trust the Lord and told the head teacher that he would be absent on Saturdays. However, the final exam was on a Saturday, as are all exams in China. Instead of taking his exam, Alexander traveled secretly to another city to be baptized.

When his parents found out, they were furious. "You are no longer our son! Get out of the house—at once! I'll kill you and burn all your books!" The father glared at him, his eyes aflame.

"You are a shame to me!" yelled his mother. "You'll drive me to kill myself." Shaking and bewildered, Alexander backed away from his parents and then ran for his life.

He expected his college to throw him out too. They didn't. He simply received a polite letter saying he could take his exams at the beginning of the next term. He was amazed, and his parents tolerated his return home. The next term, he had new teachers and six hours of classes on Sabbath. He didn't attend these. Then weeks later, Alexander went to tell his new head teacher about his nonattendance. The teacher was furious. "I'll have you severely punished if you do not come," he shouted. You are a trouble maker; that's all you are!" Alexander trembled but continued to skip Sabbath classes. By then, every student in the university knew he was a Sabbath keeper. "Stop this foolishness! Conform!" students taunted and urged.

One day, two of his teachers visited his home, some distance from the school, a highly unusual thing for Chinese teachers to do.

"You are very foolish, stubborn, and insubordinate!" ranted one.

"Delinquent and a trouble maker too," yelled the other. They denounced him in front of his parents. "The faculty will meet soon and decide your fate. You will be disciplined harshly!" Then they abruptly left.

"You utterly good-for-nothing." The father shook him hard. "You disgrace our name! You must obey your teachers or suffer the consequences!"

A deep dread and darkness descended over Alexander. He crept away and spent the entire week in fasting and prayer. His finals were coming in two weeks. What should he do? He was scared to look at the published exam schedule on the notice board. He scanned the dates. His classes were the only ones not scheduled for Saturday! Christ had not forgotten this teenager in China. "Thank You, Christ! Oh, thank You!" Alexander exclaimed. "God is faithful, who will not allow you to be tempted beyond what you are able, but with the temptation will also make the way of escape, that you may be able to bear it" (1 Corinthians 10:13, NKJV). Praise the Lord!

Recently, Alexander graduated. He plans to be an evangelist to the poor provinces in the north of China. Let's pray for him. Today, many Seventh-day Adventists, like Alexander, suffer for their Sabbath convictions. They have entered the early time of trouble ahead of us.

Life after the Sunday law

Persecution is coming to the rest of us soon. We will confront the end-time Sunday laws. They will put us to the test. Proposals to change the Constitution are aired much today. Nothing is new. In the 1880s, similar efforts were made. We read, "Those who are making an effort to change the Constitution and secure a law enforcing Sunday observance little realize what will be the result. A crisis is just upon us" (1889).[1] God held the winds in check (Revelation 7:1-4). But they are loosening today. This is end time.

Amidst the plethora of media sex and crime, family values are discussed by many Christians and legislators. With the stunning victory of the Republican party in November 1994, the Christian Coalition is working hard behind the scenes to take over the White House and make America a Christian nation. They have unprecedented influence on Congress. Where are we headed?

God's end-time picture of America is a country that outwardly professes to be Christian and concerned about moral issues— the very agenda of the Christian Coalition. Ellen White foresaw that Christian organizations would claim that "the fast-spreading corruption is largely attributable to the desecration of the so-called 'Christian sabbath,' and that the enforcement of Sunday observance would greatly improve the morals of society."[2] But many Americans are not Christians. Will they support this view?

Satan is busy influencing public opinion. "Satan puts his interpretation upon events, and they [Americans] think, as he would have them, that the calamities which fill the land are a result of Sundaybreaking. Thinking to appease the wrath of God these influential men make laws enforcing Sunday observance."[3] Can they carry the country? God says, "Political corruption is destroying love of justice and regard for truth; and even in free America, rulers and legislators, in order to secure public favor, will yield to the popular demand for a law enforcing Sunday observance."[4] So it becomes the popular view, and legislation follows.

And who is the major player behind this decision? "When the leading churches of the United States, uniting upon such points of doctrine as are held by them in common, shall influence the state to enforce their decrees and to sustain their institutions, then Protestant America will have formed an image of the Roman hierarchy, and the infliction of civil penalties upon dissenters will inevitably result."[5] It is a Christian initiative— a Christian coalition.

For God or country?

William J. Bennett, in his *The Book of Virtues*, says, "The times when one cannot stand both 'for God and for country' are rare indeed."[6] When the Sunday law is passed, such a time will have arrived. "Our country [America] shall repudiate every principle of its Constitution as a Protestant and republican government." Then "the time has come for the marvelous working of Satan and . . . the end is near."[7] "The Sabbath question is to be the issue in the great final conflict in which all the world will act a part."[8] It "will agitate the whole world."[9]

Think of the paradox: God's people will be required by law to break the moral law (the Sabbath). They will be accused of the very thing the legislators are doing. They will be "denounced as enemies of law and order, as breaking down the moral restraints of society, causing anarchy and corruption, and calling down the judgments of God upon the earth."[10] Where will this lead to? "Because of our advocacy of Bible truth, we shall be treated as traitors."[11] Those loyal to God, and therefore to the best interests of their countries, will be scandalized as traitors! Actually, those promoting laws are the traitors—to God and country. "Those who are true to God will be persecuted, their motives will be impugned, their best efforts misrepresented, and their names cast out as evil."[12]

"As the defenders of truth refuse to honor the Sunday-sabbath, some of them will be thrust into prison, some will be exiled, some will be treated as slaves. To human wisdom all this now seems impossible; but as the restraining Spirit of God shall be withdrawn from men, and they shall be under the control of Satan, who hates the divine precepts, there will be strange developments. The heart can be very cruel when God's fear and love are removed."[13]

The time of the latter rain

To focus only on Sunday laws is to look at Satan's work. But Christ is at work too. At the precise time Satan obtains Sunday laws, Christ sends the latter rain—His powerful presence—to be with His people. The world may forsake us. But Christ will not. "Never will I leave you; never will I forsake you" (Hebrews

13:5) is His pledge of loyalty to those who remain loyal to Him. We will then enter a period similar to the early-church period. Ellen White says, "Study carefully in the book of Acts the experiences of Paul and the other apostles, for God's people in our day must pass through similar experiences."[14]

I believe that some of the events recorded in the book of Acts will be repeated around the world in the early time of trouble. Most of the book follows Pentecost, just as the early time of trouble follows the coming Pentecost. Before Pentecost, the disciples, in the upper room, were seeking the highest place in Christ's kingdom. This happens too often today in local churches and beyond. People want control. This began in the heart of Lucifer. The early time of trouble is Satan's final bid to gain control of the planet. We must not be like him. We must be like Christ, who gave up everything at the risk of failure to come to this rebel planet. He emptied Himself of His absolute authority and became a helpless baby and a dependent human for you (Philippians 2:5-11). What a contrast—Satan wanted to become God, and God became a human!

In the other upper room, praying for the Holy Spirit, proud disciples became humble followers of Christ. How? The memory of Christ broke their proud hearts. His death cast their pride in the dust. "As they meditated upon His pure, holy life they felt that no toil would be too hard, no sacrifice too great, if only they could bear witness in their lives to the loveliness of Christ's character. . . . The disciples prayed with intense earnestness for a fitness to meet men and in their daily intercourse to speak words that would lead sinners to Christ. Putting away all differences, all desire for the supremacy, they came close together in Christian fellowship."[15] Seeking supremacy was cheap in the light of the One who gave up everything for them.

It will happen again. "The people of God will draw together and present to the enemy a united front. In view of the common peril, strife for supremacy will cease; there will be no disputing as to who shall be accounted greatest."[16] As we see events leading to the Sunday law, we need self to be crucified now. The disciples were humble men before Pentecost. Without humility, we cannot receive the latter rain. So many today criticize the church and its leaders. Whose spirit do they have? Remember, it is Satan who is angry with the church (Revelation 12:17), for in the end time it keeps him from absolute supremacy of the world. By contrast, "God's love for His church is infinite."[17]

No critic will receive the latter rain. It is time to press together, press together, and with earnest seeking open our hearts to be softened by the Holy Spirit. We need the fullness of the Holy Spirit to be ready for the latter rain. If career, position, or status are uppermost in our hearts, it is because we have not gazed at Christ hanging on Calvary for us. What does it profit if we gain the whole world (as Satan is attempting) and loose our own souls (Matthew 16:26)? Show me a man or a woman who spends time each day meditating on the depths of Calvary, and there you have a candidate for Pentecost.

In the apostolic church, God's people were filled with the Holy Spirit (Acts 4:8, 31; 6:3; 7:55; 8:17; 10:44, 45; 11:15, 22-24; 13:9), who is the One called "the Spirit of Jesus" (Acts 16:7), and the Spirit led them (Acts 8:29, 39; 9:31; 10:19; 13:2; 15:28; 16:6, 7; 20:22, 28), as well as the angel of the Lord (Acts 8:26; 27:23). They had visions (Acts 9:10-16; 10:1-7, 9-23; 18:9; 22:17, 18). Just as the Holy Spirit comes to glorify Christ (John 16:13, 14), so the Spirit-filled apostles preached about Jesus—His life, death, and resurrection (Acts 2:22-36; 3:13-21; 4:10-12; 5:30, 31, 42; 7:52; 8:35; 9:22; 11:20; 13:23-39; 28:23). The apostles had courage (Acts 4:13) and spoke boldly (Acts 4:31), and people took note that "these men had been with Jesus" (Acts 4:13). In the end time, God's people will have courage and boldness because Jesus is with them too (Matthew 28:20). They will present Christ in relationship to His Sabbath. The call to follow Christ (Revelation 18:4) will be seen in the light of accepting Him as "Lord . . . of the Sabbath" (Mark 2:28).

There were imprisonments (Acts 4:3; 12:4-10; 16:22-31), confinement to barracks (Acts 23:10), floggings (Acts 5:40; 16:23; 21:32), stoning (Acts 14:19), and two martyrs (Stephen, Acts 7:54-60; and James the brother of John, Acts 12:2). But Christ was with His people. God rescued them from prison (Acts 12:4-10; 16:22-31). "The apostles performed many miraculous signs and wonders" (Acts 5:12). Cripples walked again (Acts 3:1-7; 14:8-10), evil spirits were cast out (Acts 5:16), and Tabitha (Acts 9:36-40) and Eutychus (Acts 20:7-10) were raised from the dead, These events can happen again around the world.

Recently, a student in my last-day events class blurted out, "I want to die before the Sunday law and go to heaven via resurrection." This was near the beginning of the semester. Yes, I would, too, if I looked at the crisis instead of to Christ. It was the memory of Christ that compelled disciples to be bold and to face any danger. The Holy Spirit took away their fear. Those who live through the last days will have an experience that those who died will miss. They will be sealed (Revelation 7:1-4), filled with the latter rain (James 5:7), and receiving visions or dreams (Joel 2:28, 29). When they get to heaven, they will praise Christ for the privilege of living through last-day events.

Think what may happen. The Spirit of Christ will guide us in vision to go to certain houses and bring them the Sabbath truth. People will see visions of these truth bearers coming. The Holy Spirit guided this way in Acts (9:10-16; 10:1-7, 9-23). The saved will give the invitation for others to come out and join them (Revelation 18:4). Many will gladly respond and share their food when we cannot buy or sell (Revelation 13:17).

In the early church, the members went from house to house (Acts 5:42). During the final message, "servants of God, with their faces lighted up and shining with holy consecration, will hasten from place to place to proclaim the message from heaven. By thousands of voices, all over the earth, the warning will be given. Miracles will be wrought, the sick will be healed, and signs and wonders will follow the believers. . . . The message will be carried not so much by argument as by the deep conviction of the Spirit of God."[18]

Our greatest need

Even some leaders will never receive the latter rain. They will resist it because it does not come according to their expectations (E. G. White, *Review and Herald*, 7 November 1918). Could I be in that group? It is not *what we have done*, but *who we are* that counts. It is not *what position or knowledge* we have that is essential, but *who we know* (John 17:3). We all need to pray earnestly for the Spirit of Christ in latter-rain power to flood our lives and set us free to be used in the end time. Laodicea is blind and does not know it (Revelation 3:17-20). Her blindness is due to keeping Christ outside her life. When Christ comes within a person, He brings discernment. We receive the gift with the Giver, and not without. Where Christ is, there is freedom. My friend Jeris Bragan, locked up in the penitentiary, puts it well: "They can take away my liberty, but not my freedom in Christ." So it will be in final events.

Christ's people will be so filled with His Spirit that they will reflect His love, His righteousness. "The last message of mercy to be given to the world, is a revelation of His character and love. The children of God are to manifest His glory. In their own life and character they are to reveal what the grace of God has done for them."[19] We need to pray for a burden for those who need to hear the message. Then compassion for them will overcome fear of final events. Besides, "it is the latter rain which revives and strengthens them to pass through the time of trouble."[20]

Friend, be done with fear of final events. Be open to the latter rain. God's Spirit will give you boldness beyond your wildest imagination. Dare for Christ. If you look at the papacy and its rule of the planet with an enforced Sunday law, you are looking in the wrong direction, and you will experience fear. But look to the latter rain and the coming Christ in deliverance, and you will find yourself liberated from your fears. Those filled with the latter rain will be hated by nearly everyone, but they will be the freest people in the world. They will know the truth about the ultimate outcome. They will be on the winning side, and they already have some of the future in the present, through the mighty indwelling of the Spirit of Christ.

---

1. *Last Day Events*, 126.
2. *The Great Controversy*, 587.
3. *Last Day Events*, 129.
4. *The Great Controversy*, 592.
5. *Last Day Events*, 131.

6. *The Book of Virtues*, 666.
7. *Testimonies for the Church*, 5:451.
8. Ibid., 6:352.
9. Ellen G. White, *Evangelism*, 236.
10. *The Great Controversy*, 592.
11. *Testimonies for the Church*, 6:394.
12. Ellen G. White, *The Acts of the Apostles*, 431.
13. *The Great Controversy*, 608.
14. *Last Day Events*, 148.
15. *The Acts of the Apostles*, 36, 37.
16. *Testimonies for the Church*, 6:401.
17. Ibid., 9:228.
18. *The Great Controversy*, 612.
19. Ellen G. White, *Christ's Object Lessons*, 415, 416.
20. Ellen G. White Comments, *SDA Bible Commentary*, 7:984.

Chapter 11

Christ
and the 144,000

As never before, the world is impacting Christians and secularizing churches. What kind of world is it? Take America, for example. The population of America has increased 41 percent since 1960. "But during that time there has been a 560 percent increase in violent crimes; a 419 percent increase in illegitimate births, a quadrupling in divorce rates; a tripling of the percentage of children living in single parent homes; more than 200 percent increase in teenage suicides; and a drop of almost 80 points in the SAT scores."[1]

H. B. London, assistant to Dr. James C. Dobson, and Neil B. Wiseman, vice-president for academics at Nazarene Bible College in Colorado Springs, Colorado, co-authored a book, *Pastors at Risk*, in 1993. Focus on the Family wrote to five thousand pastors from their mailing list of seventy-seven thousand pastors. This is what they found. "Pastors are frustrated because people seem apathetic."[2] "Pastors deal daily with diluted dedication, family disintegration, superficial commitments, and an accepted churchly consumerism no longer interested in sacrifice, suffering, or servanthood."[3] About 40 percent of pastors say they have considered giving up the ministry.[4]

Fuller Theological Seminary's Institute of Church Growth conducted a survey of pastors in 1991 and found some disturbing facts. Eighty percent believe that pastoral ministry affects their families negatively, 33 percent said that being in ministry is an outright hazard to their family, 75 percent reported a significant stress-related crisis at least once in their ministry, 50 percent feel unable to meet the needs of the job, 70 percent report a lower self-esteem now than when they started out, 70 percent do not have someone they consider a close friend, and 40 percent reported a serious conflict with a parishioner at least once a month.[5]

A church at risk

There's a great war going on. Satan is changing churches to be like the world. Is he succeeding in our church too? One thing is certain: ours is the only church that Scripture states Satan is mad at (Revelation 12:17). He is like a roaring lion seeking to devour (1 Peter 5:8). We can expect his anger to be felt in the church even more as we move to the end time, when apostate churches follow him in the Sunday issue. He sees in this church the one obstacle in the way of his world domination. So now he works fiendishly to destroy Seventh-day Adventists, to impart to them his spirit of criticism, harshness, and selfishness. If the majority will leave the church at the time the Sunday law is enacted,[6] we dare not compare our Christianity with other members.' *God has His end-time saints in every church.*

Christ says, "Standard after standard was left to trail in the dust as company after company from the Lord's army joined the foe and tribe after tribe from the ranks of the enemy united with the commandment-keeping people of God."[7]

Christ is looking for people from every church who love Him above all else and love their fellow humans too. Those who walk in His presence and have eternal things in focus. Those who practice servanthood in the church, who refuse to see the bad and look for the good. Those who talk more with Christ and refuse to gossip. Those who realize they have but one life and want to be a blessing to all they contact. Those who live for Christ and long to do His will, who earnestly seek His guidance and totally depend upon Him. Those who know God loves them, not because they are good, but because He is good. Those who know Christ treats them, not as they deserve, but as they need. Those who gratefully let Christ love through them in the same way. These constitute the church of the end time.

God says, "In the last solemn work few great men will be engaged. . . . God will work a work in our day that but few anticipate. He will raise up and exalt among us those who are taught rather by the unction of His Spirit than by the outward training of scientific institutions. . . . God will manifest that He is not dependent on learned, self-important mortals."[8]

Christ's end-time saints

These end-time saints, who will go through final events and be translated, are called the 144,000. This is a name rather than a number. How do we know? Consider Revelation 7:9, 10, 13, 14. The group that comes out of the great tribulation (great time of trouble, Daniel 12:1) are "a great multitude that no one could count," and they come "from every nation, tribe, people and language." So the translated group will be made up of people from around the world, not just from the twelve Hebrew tribes listed in Revelation 7.

We will study Revelation 14, a crucial chapter for Seventh-day Adventists because of the three angels' messages (verses 6-13). We are first introduced to the 144,000 standing with the Lamb (Christ) on Mount Zion. Where is this scene, and when does it take place? In the Old Testament, Mt. Zion is the dwelling place of God, Jerusalem (Psalms 74:2), the place of deliverance (Joel 2:32). In the New Testament, Mt. Zion is "the heavenly Jerusalem, the city of the living God" (Hebrews 12:22), which will come to the new earth for eternity (Revelation 21:1-3). So the 144,000 are seen standing with Christ either in heaven, during the millennium, or after the millennium on the new earth. Verse 4 says, "They follow the Lamb wherever he goes," and this seems to point to the eternal future. We will need to return to this later.

We are told that the 144,000 sing a new song that only they can sing (verse 3). Only these saints pass through the great time of trouble and are translated. This song is "the song of their experience—an experience such as no other company have ever had."[9] These are the ones who live after the close of probation, after Christ completes His intercession in heaven (Daniel 12:1). Here they stand with the Lamb. This is significant, for only they and the Lamb have lived after the close of probation. Christ, as it were, lived His whole human life after the close of probation. There would have been no Saviour interceding in heaven for Him if He had sinned.

Why are they standing together? Or, to put it another way, why does this group follow Christ wherever He goes throughout eternity?

Mission of the 144,000

After the Sunday laws, there follows a little time of trouble during which the final invitation is made for people to stand with God's saints. The Sabbath issue is global. Prime-time news via satellite will make *Adventist* a household word. Seventh-day Adventists' refusal to comply with Sunday legislation will be the lead story. People will be confronted with a choice, to obey God or humans. Those who are already "my people," says Christ (Revelation 18:4), will join Seventh-day Adventists in their stand and become a significant part of the 144,000.

When everyone has voted for or against the Sabbath, then the close of probation will take place. Time will be given so that all can intelligently make their own decision, and then the work of evangelization will be forever finished. Those giving the loud-cry invitation under the power of the latter rain will be sealed and thus ready for translation. Then why does not the second advent take place at the close of probation? Why the great time of trouble? Why would a God of love require that His translation people remain on earth to go through the worst time of trouble ever? There must be an important reason. There is. It has to do with an important issue in the great controversy.

Satan has always charged that God made a law that cannot be kept (DA 761; PP 69). In other words, angels and humans who have broken His law shouldn't be blamed for breaking the law. They were made factory imperfect by Christ (see Hebrews 1:2), and so Christ is to be blamed. God's justice is on the line. It is true that Christ became a dependent human and lived the law perfectly, showing that Adam could have done the same. But many people believe that Christ lived on earth as God, not as a man.

This confusion is nothing new. Back in AD 325, the Council of Nicaea proclaimed that Jesus Christ was fully God and fully man. But the decisions rendered did not explain the relationship between His two natures. In the sixteenth century, Martin Luther taught that the two natures were so scrambled together within Christ that He was a third type of being, neither fully divine nor fully human. Luther believed that Christ's humanity was permeated with His own divinity and that such a being is incapable of sinning. Luther's contemporary, John Calvin, taught that the divinity of Christ remained omnipresent during His human life so that He was at the throne of heaven even while being tempted as a human. If either Luther's or Calvin's position is correct, Christ had an advantage over other human beings, and His perfect life did not answer Satan's charge that normal human beings were incapable of keeping God's law. In fact, if Christ needed such an advantage to enable Him to obey, this would validate Satan's charge.

Add to this the fact that all humans who have ever lived will live again at the end of the millennium. We can imagine that the end-time generation, who live during the final events and beyond probation's close, could cry out, "God, You are not fair! We were the weakest of the race, living under the most trying circumstances. How could we have kept Your law?" In response, Jesus will be able to point to the 144,000 and say, "These were your contemporaries. With My help, they kept all the commandments of God" (see Revelation 12:17).

The mission of the 144,000 is to help answer the charge against Christ in the great controversy. They are asked to remain on earth during the greatest time of trouble to show that the weakest of the race during the most trying circumstances can keep God's commandments when filled with His Spirit and totally dependent upon Him. They will come from every nation, kindred, tongue, and people. These sealed saints testify that Christ was able to keep them from falling and to present them before His glorious presence without fault and with great joy (Jude 24). This is why every knee will bow and every tongue confess that God is just and Satan's charge is false.

Experience of the 144,000

This group will go through all final events: the enactment of the Sunday law; the great time of trouble, when the death decree will be issued against those who persist in faithfulness to God and His law; and the time of Jacob's trouble. Despite these many trials, the redeemed will sing about this experience during and after the millennium. That's incredible! Do you sing about your bad times, or do you try to forget them? Here is a crucial point to those who are scared of final events—*if it's worth singing about so long after the experience, it must be worth going through!*

The song they sing is given in Revelation 15:3 and 4. Notice the focus. "Great and marvelous are your deeds, Lord God Almighty. Just and true are your ways, King of the ages." The focus is on what Christ has done for them and against their enemies. They are like the three Hebrew worthies in the fiery furnace. The life-preserving presence of Christ in the flames with them has transformed the crisis into something worth singing about. Their song is of Christ, not about themselves. There is no word about their not sinning, about their contribution to the great-controversy issue. They are in awe of Christ. "For you alone are holy. All nations will come and worship before you, for your righteous acts have been revealed" (verse 4). They have seen the plagues and the battle of Armageddon. They have something worth singing about forever, as together with the Lamb they go from planet to planet to speak of their experience.

How to get into the 144,000

Did you ever wonder why the verses about the 144,000 (Revelation 14:1-5) precede those about the three angels' messages (verses 6-13)? The three messages prepare a person to be in the group. Space will only allow a brief recap of these messages. The first calls us to look to Christ, particularly in the judgment hour. Looking to Christ brings change (2 Corinthians 3:18). The first angel calls us to become like Christ. The second angel speaks of Babylon's fall. The Tower of Babel, and later Babylon, represents self-dependence. Put the two together. If we gaze on Christ and become changed, self-dependence will crumble. The third speaks about the image to the beast. Historically, the beast is the papacy, or the union of church and state. Such a union in America will image the papacy, in which secular power is used to enforce a religious law (Sunday). Experientially, this is trying to be religious in one's own secular power (for that is all one has apart from Christ).

Putting the three messages together, they say, Beholding Christ brings change, so that self-dependence crumbles, even to the extent that one no longer tries to be religious in their own secular power. Truly this is righteousness by faith. It is total dependence upon Christ alone. It is a helplessness that clings to Christ during Jacob's trouble as Jacob did during his night of wrestling (Genesis 32:26). It is a total giving up on ourselves, which is necessary before Christ can finish His own work and keep us alive in the flames of the final fiery furnace.

The other three angels of Revelation 14

There are six angels in Revelation 14. Three have a message (verses 6-13), and three have a mission (verses 14-20). We will look into this mission when we study the battle of Armageddon. This much we can say now. The wicked will be destroyed and God's saints delivered. This must be remembered. Christ will have the last word. Some study final events and look at the Sunday law, death decree, and time of Jacob's trouble and forget the rest of the story—the outcome of it all. It is bad news for those who enact the Sunday law and death decree. To be on their side in the end is to have something to be fearful about. Some Christians are afraid of final events, as if they expect to be on the losing side.

The final exodus

The new song that the 144,000 sing is called "the song of Moses the servant of God and the song of the Lamb" (Revelation 15:3). When Moses stood with the children of Israel at the Red Sea, it looked like uncrossable water ahead of them, with an unbeatable army pushing from behind. What were they to do? "They were terrified and cried out to the Lord" (Exodus

14:10). It was then that God provided deliverance. The people could not take any credit. God spoke through Moses, "The Lord will fight for you; you need only to be still" (verse 14). He caused confusion among the Egyptians and made their chariot wheels come off so that even the Egyptians said, "The Lord is fighting for them against Egypt" (verse 25).

The Egyptian army was totally destroyed and God's people totally delivered. That gave them something to sing about! Exodus 15:1-18 records their praise and thanksgiving in the song of Moses. "In your unfailing love you will lead the people you have redeemed. In your strength you will guide them to your holy dwelling" (verse 13). This exodus is a type of the global exodus through final events. As the Israelites escaped from Egypt and passed through the threat of death on their way to the land of promise, so the 144,000 will escape from Babylon and its death decree and cross over unharmed to the heavenly land of promise.

To those living in the last days, the Sunday law will be like the Red Sea was to the Israelites. We will feel helpless. Not just an army but the whole world will be against us (Revelation 13:3, 15). The experience of the three angels' messages will be ours. We will have given up on trying to do anything to save ourselves. Our trust will be in Christ alone. And He will fight the battle for us and open up a way through final events. This is what the 144,000 will sing about as they sing the song of Moses and the song of the Lamb.

Behind both days of deliverance is that greater deliverance at Calvary, where Christ took our place and perished, as it were, in the Red Sea for us so that we could go over on dry ground. For He came to die for all the redeemed, and death is something the 144,000 will never experience. What a future! This is our finest hour. Let's look beyond the passing scene in our church to that glorious rendezvous with destiny. For this hour we were born. Let us look to Christ and not to the crisis. Then we will experience the triumph that we can sing about for eternity. If this time of trial and deliverance is worth singing about forever, it must be a time worth going through!

1. William J. Bennett, "Cultural Indicators Chart our Moral Climate," *Colorado Springs Gazette*, 28 March 1993, section D, 5. Quoted in H. B. London, Jr., and Neil B. Wiseman, *Pastors at Risk* (Wheaton, Ill.: Victor Books, 1993), 42.
2. *Pastors at Risk*, 25
3. Ibid., 29.
4. Ibid., 25.
5. Ibid., 22.
6. *Last Day Events*, 180. See also 172–182.
7. *Testimonies for the Church*, 8:41.
8. *Testimonies for the Church*, 5:80, 82.
9. *The Great Controversy*, 649.

Chapter 12

Christ
and Satan's Lie

It was in the middle of the night. He lay in bed. Suddenly, he awakened to the sense that someone else was in the room. A lonely widower, he longed for the companionship of his deceased wife. His eyes opened, and there she walked, the appearance of his beloved companion coming to his bedside.

"My darling, I have come to see you. Oh, how I miss you!" He was wide awake by now. She looked exactly like his wife. The long, flowing hair; those deep blue eyes; that melodious voice. She used an endearing name for him that only the two of them knew. His emotions stirred to the depths; his mind whirled; then he snapped out of it. "I know you are not my wife," he choked "I bid you in the name of Jesus Christ, begone!" And the being left the room. Depressed, he turned over and wept. What a cruel and cheap counterfeit. He knew that his wife could not return and speak to him from the grave.

"Many will be confronted by the spirits of devils personating beloved relatives or friends and declaring the most dangerous heresies. These visitants will appeal to our tenderest sympathies and will work miracles to sustain their pretensions."[1] "These manifestations will be more frequent, and developments of a more startling character will appear as we near the close of time."[2]

"Evil angels come in the form of those loved ones and relate incidents connected with their lives, and perform acts which they performed while living. In this way they lead persons to believe that their dead friends are angels, hovering over them and com-

municating with them. These evil angels, who assume to be the
deceased friends, are regarded with a certain idolatry, and with
many their word has greater weight than the Word of God."[3]

Spiritualism

Satan said in Eden, "You will not surely die" (Genesis 3:4).
"Through the two great errors, the immortality of the soul and
Sunday sacredness, Satan will bring the people under his decep-
tions. While the former lays the foundation of spiritualism, the
latter creates a bond of sympathy with Rome. The Protestants of
the United States will be foremost in stretching their hands across
the gulf to grasp the hand of spiritualism; they will reach over the
abyss to clasp hands with the Roman power; and under the influence of this threefold union, this country will follow in the steps of
Rome in trampling on the rights of conscience."[4] "Satan determines to unite them in one body and thus strengthen his cause by
sweeping all into the ranks of spiritualism."[5]

The Catholic Church "has clothed herself in Christlike garments; but she is unchanged,"[6] and spiritualism "is assuming
a Christian guise."[7] "Satan has long been preparing for his final effort to deceive the world. . . . Little by little he has prepared the way for his masterpiece of deception in the development of spiritualism."[8] "Except those who are kept by the power
of God, through faith in His word, the whole world will be swept
into the ranks of this delusion. The people are fast being lulled
to a fatal security."[9] "Through spiritualism, Satan appears as a
benefactor of the race . . . professing to present a new and more
exalted system of religious faith,"[10] as he did in heaven.[11]

Views on death

Karl Barth, one of the most influential theologians of the
twentieth century, believed death was a part of God's original
plan for the human race. He contrasts God, who has no beginning and no end, with humans, who had a beginning and must
necessarily have an end. This was a part of his emphasis that
God is wholly other than humankind. Thus human death was
ordained by God even if humans had not sinned.[12] (This is not
a new view. It was held by Celestius in the fifth century AD

and by the Socinians from the sixteenth century onward.)[13]

Evolutionary theory suggests that humans are the latest development in the long line of ascendancy. Before humans arrived, there were countless deaths of animals over a vast time span. This is accepted by Christian thinkers.[14] By contrast, the Bible says that "the wages of sin is death" (Romans 6:23), that "death came through a man" (1 Corinthians 15:21), and that "sin entered the world through one man, and death through sin" (Romans 5:12). For death is linked with God's judgment (Revelation 2:11; 20:6; 21:8).

Romans 5 compares Adam and Christ (Christ is called "the last Adam" in 1 Corinthians 15:45). In opposite ways, each "Adam" made a contribution to death. Romans 5:12-19 is a parallelism, noting the gifts to the race made by each "Adam." Just as one sin (verse 16), "one trespass" (verse 5:18), brought condemnation and death to the whole race, so "one act . . . brings life for all" (verse 18). The one act of the second Adam, His death, canceled the result of the one act of the first Adam (verse 10). So Christ's death destroyed the one who "holds the power of death" (Hebrews 2:14) and "destroyed death" (2 Timothy 1:10). Death could not hold Him (Acts 2:24), so Christ is now said to be "Lord of both the dead and the living" (Romans 14:9) who "has the keys of death and Hades" (Revelation 1:18)."[15]

The New Testament speaks of Christ as the firstborn (in importance, not time) from the dead (Colossians 1:18; Revelation 1:5). It claims that death does not "separate us" from Christ (Romans 8:38, 39). It can even say that death is being "at home with the Lord" (2 Corinthians 5:8), is "gain" (Philippians 1:21), and is "to depart and be with Christ" (Philippians 1:23) as well as to have "fallen asleep" (John 11:11). What are these passages attempting to say? Is death for the saints an immediate entrance into heaven or a cessation of existence till the resurrection in the end time?

Immortality

In the *Phaedo* of Plato (ca. 427-347 BC), Socrates philosophizes about death before he drinks the poison. Death is defined as "a release and separation from the body" (67.D, compare 66.E). For the "soul is immortal" (*athanaton*, 73.A). In life, the soul is "entirely fastened and welded to the body and is compelled to regard realities through the body as through prison bars" (82.E). The soul, therefore, is "never willingly associated with the body" (80.E, compare "hostile to the body," 67.E). So at death the soul is "freed from the body as from fetters" (67.D). To be afraid to die is to love the body more than wisdom (68.B.C.). In facing his own death, Socrates had no fear and looked forward to the release. He took the hemlock "very cheerfully and quietly drained it" (*Phaedo* 117.C).[16]

In his incisive book *Immortality of the Soul or Resurrection of the Dead*, New Testament scholar Oscar Cullman begins his introduction as follows. "If we were to ask an ordinary Christian today (whether well-read Protestant or Catholic, or not) what he conceived to be the New Testament teaching concerning the fate of man after death, with few exceptions we should get the answer: 'The immortality of the soul.' Yet this widely-accepted idea is one of the greatest misunderstandings of Christianity" (London, U.K.: Epworth, 1958, 15). How true. Of all our fundamental beliefs, this is the one that is often the hardest to teach non-Adventists. They believe their loved ones are in heaven and gain comfort from this.

In Scripture, immortality is never an innate quality. Rather, it is something to be sought after (Romans 2:7) and is a gift (Romans 6:23). Humans are always said to be mortal (Romans 6:12; 8:11; 1 Corinthians 15:53, 54; 2 Corinthians 4:11; 5:4).[17] Through His death, Christ "has brought life and immortality to light through the gospel" (2 Timothy 1:10).

The biblical worldview

The biblical worldview is the crucial context within which we must grapple with the texts that on the surface seem to teach an immediate survival after death. That worldview includes three fundamental facts. (1) God "alone is immortal" (1 Timothy 6:16). (2) Not until the second advent will the saints receive immortality, and death will be "swallowed up in victory" (1 Corinthians 15:54). For, (3) "The last enemy to be destroyed is death" (1 Corinthians 15:26). Clearly, Scripture points humans to a future hope of immortality and to overcoming death as an enemy and not to their own personal survival at death. The immortality-of-the-soul doctrine completely overlooks this future dimension. But it also overlooks the past dimension, that is, the nature of humans as created.

Some Christian thinkers claim that humans are immortal because they were created in the image or likeness of God (Genesis 1:26, 27). For example, John Calvin said, "The first man had an immortal soul."[18] They suggest that the text about only God having immortality merely refers to the eternal past. Obviously, as created beings, humans cannot claim to have immortality in the past. However, through creation, they argue, humans were gifted with innate immortality. But those who reason thus overlook Scripture's own definition of the image or likeness of God. Image or likeness, to some extent, seems to suggest physical appearance rather than eternal existence. Further, it was as male and female that the first humans imaged the Godhead. As the members of the Trinity relate to each other as equals, though having different functions, so did Adam and Eve (Genesis 1:27). They were given dominion over the world that images God's dominion over the universe. Nowhere does Scripture say that humans were given immortality.

It was God who said in Eden, eat the fruit and "you will die" (Genesis 3:3). It was Satan who said, "You will not surely die" (verse 4). God took death seriously. Satan countered with a false view of immortality. God gave an important insight into human mortality after the Fall. He said, "The man has now become like one of us, knowing good and evil. He must not be allowed to reach out his hand and take also from the tree of life and eat, and live forever" (verse 22). Clearly, humans could not be innately immortal, or this prohibition would be meaningless.

No soul/body separation

Nowhere in Scripture is a person less than a union of soul and body. When God said to Adam and Eve that they would die if they sinned, He did not mean, *Your body will die, but your soul will live forever*. Richard L. Purtill notes, "In the past few decades a good many able philosophers have become convinced that there are new and decisive objections to the notion of disembodied survival."[19]

Nowhere in Scripture is there a description of an intermediate state between a person's death and resurrection. In fact, there is no disparity between an individual's end in death and the cosmic end in resurrection at the second advent (1 Corinthians 15:51-55) or after the millennium (Revelation 20:5). The body remains in the grave until the resurrection. The resurrected do not meet Christ before the translated. They meet Christ in the second advent (1 Thessalonians 4:16-18).

In the New Testament, there are three major resurrections that call into question the idea that a person goes straight to heaven at death. First, Lazarus was resurrected after being buried for four days (John 11:17). If a person goes in death to be with God, then Christ did Lazarus a disservice to resurrect him to mundane life in this world.

Second, in Christ's death, the earth shook, and tombs were broken open, and "many holy people who had died were raised to life" (Matthew 27:51-53). They lived on earth for forty days, and when Christ "ascended on high, he led [these] captives in his train" (Ephesians 4:7). As in the case of Enoch (Genesis 5:24; Hebrews 11:5), Elijah (2 Kings 2:11), and Moses (Matthew 17:3; Jude 9), these are exceptions to the rule that the dead remain asleep until the cosmic resurrections. The very fact that they are mentioned shows that it is not a normal thing to go to be with God in death.

The third resurrection is Christ's. He remained in the grave until the third day. The proof that He did not ascend to be with God the moment He died is found in His words to Mary on Sunday morning. He said, "Do not hold on to me, for I have not yet returned to the Father" (John 20:17). These words of Christ guide us in properly interpreting His words to the dying thief, "I tell you the truth, today you will be with me in paradise" (Luke 23:43). Where is paradise? The Greek word for "paradise" (*paradeisos*) occurs only in Luke 23:43; 2 Corinthians 12:4, and Revelation 2:7 and is a synonym for heaven. So Jesus could not have said to the thief, "You will be with Me in heaven to-day," when He told Mary two days later, "I have not yet returned to heaven."

Other texts

It would take a book to adequately evaluate arguments for immediate life with Christ at death. There is a biblical principle to guide this quest. Any texts that apparently suggest an immediate survival at death must be evaluated against the context of the biblical worldview we have described above. Then apparent exceptions will be seen as such, for the Bible does not have contradictory views. Let's apply this principle. What did Paul mean when he said he would prefer to be "away from the body" and be "at home with the Lord" (2 Corinthians 5:8)? What did he mean when he said, "I desire to depart and be with Christ" (Philippians 1:23)? This is the same Paul who states that the resurrected saints meet Christ in the air at the second advent, and not at death (1 Thessalonians 4:16-18). It should be remembered that the moment the saints close their eyes in death, the very next instant, for them, is the resurrection to be with Christ at the second advent.

What about the parable of the rich man and Lazarus (Luke 16:19-31)? This is a favorite passage for those supporting continuance of life at death. It is important to note that parables "teach one fundamental truth," and the details are of no doctrinal significance.[20] The important thing to remember is that doctrines are derived from prescriptive passages from Scripture and not from descriptive passages. (This is why the fourth commandment is a more important source for which day is the Sabbath than any first-day meetings of Christians.)

Paul affirms that death, among other things, is unable to separate a person from the love of God (Romans 8:38, 39). No one is lost to God when they die. As Otto Kaiser and Eduard Lohse state, "Anyone who trusts in the cross of Christ . . . is not abandoned by God in death."[21] Christ's death has put death to death. Already in this life, the reality of eternal life is experienced by Christians. This is the "firstfruits [*aparche*] of the Spirit" (Romans 8:23) "as a deposit [*arrabon*], guaranteeing what is to come" (2 Corinthians 1:22). Christians have "passed from death to life" (1 John 3:14). For "whoever believes in the Son has eternal life" (John 3:36).

Spiritualism in the end time

"The doctrine of man's consciousness in death, especially the belief that spirits of the dead return to minister to the living, has prepared the way for modern spiritualism."[22] "We must be prepared to withstand them with the Bible truth that the dead know not anything and that they who thus appear are the spirits of devils. Just before us is 'the hour of temptation, which shall come upon all the world, to try them that dwell upon the earth.' Revelation 3:10. All whose faith is not firmly established upon the word of God will be deceived and overcome."[23] The biblical teaching on the state of the dead is a protection against Satan's final masterpiece of deception.

Scripture repeatedly says death is a sleep (e.g., 1 Kings 2:10; 2 Chronicles 21:1; Job 14:10-12; Jeremiah 51:39, 57; Daniel 12:2; Matthew 9:24; John 11:11-14; 1 Corinthians 15:51, 52; 1 Thessalonians 4:13-17; 2 Peter 3:4). It further says that in death "his breath goeth forth . . . ; in that very day his thoughts perish" (Psalm 146:4, KJV). "It is not the dead who praise the Lord, those who go down to silence" (Psalm 115:17). "The dead know nothing" (Ecclesiastes 9:5). "Their love, their hate and their jealousy have long since vanished" (verse 6). In the grave, "there is neither working nor planning nor knowledge nor wisdom" (verse 10). It is not until the second advent that the dead know something. They will hear Christ's voice and come forth from the grave (John 5:28, 29).

In Eden, Satan rejected Christ's warning "You shall surely die" (see Genesis 3:1-5). It seemed to Eve that the serpent had eaten of the forbidden fruit, and as a result had acquired the power of speech. He appealed to the principle "seeing is believing" (verse 6). He ate and was not dead. It worked. And it will work again in the end time when deceased loved ones appear to saints. Believing Christ about the state of the dead is seeing through Satan's counterfeit. For *believing is seeing*, a paramount need of Laodicea (Revelation 3:17, 18).

1. *The Great Controversy*, 560.

2. *Evangelism*, 604.

3. *Last Day Events*, 161.

4. *The Great Controversy*, 588.

5. Ibid., 588.

6. Ibid., 571.

7. Ibid., 557, 558.

8. Ibid., 561.

9. Ibid., 562.

10. Ibid., 589.

11. Ibid., 499.

12. Karl Barth, *Church Dogmatics* (Edinburgh: T & T Clark, 1960), 3:2, 553-572.

13. Anthony A. Hoekema, *The Bible and the Future* (Grand Rapids, Mich.: Wm. B. Eerdmans, 1979), 80.

14. Marco T. Terreos, "Death Before the Sin of Adam: A Fundamental Concept in Theistic Evolution and Its Implications for Evangelical Theology," Ph.D. Dissertation, Andrews University, 1994.

15. Norman R. Gulley, "Death: New Testament," in *The Anchor Bible Dictionary*, David Noel Freedman, editor (New York: Doubleday, 1992), 2:110.

16. Ibid., 110.

17. LeRoy Edwin Froom, *The Conditionalist Faith of Our Fathers* (Hagerstown, Md.: Review and Herald, 1966), 1:320.

18. John Calvin, *Commentary on the Epistles of Paul the Apostle to the Corinthians* (Grand Rapids, Mich.: Wm. B. Eerdmans, 1989), 20:2, 54.

19. Richard L. Purtill, "The Intelligibility of Disembodied Survival," *Christian Scholar's Review*, 5:1, 1970, 3.

20. *Seventh-day Adventist Bible Commentary* (Hagerstown, Md.: Review and Herald, 1956), 5:830.

21. Otto Kaiser and Eduard Lohse, *Death and Life* (Nashville, Tenn.: Abingdon, 1971), 115.

22. *The Great Controversy*, 551.

23. Ibid., 560.

Chapter 13

Christ
in Armageddon

How soon people forget that God is control of human affairs. Israel had already forgotten the mighty exodus. "No, we can't take this land. The giants are too tall, and we are like grasshoppers! They are stronger than us!" cried one (see Numbers 13:31-33). "They have fortified cities and are powerful and large!" yelled another (verse 28).

The bad report spread swiftly through the crowd, smothering the voices of Joshua and Caleb. "Do not be afraid of the people of the land, because we will swallow them up. Their protection is gone, but the Lord is with us. Do not be afraid of them" (Numbers 14:9).

Most looked at the giants. Few looked to God. We are about to go through last-day events to the Promised Land. Many see only giants, like Sunday laws, inability to buy or sell, the death decree, the great time of trouble, and the time of Jacob's trouble. They tremble at the crisis. Few look past the crisis to Christ, who is about to vault through the heavens on the greatest rescue mission of all times. Where are you looking?

Satan's final thrust for world domination

Giants are in the land. John speaks of them. "I saw three evil spirits that looked like frogs; they came out of the mouth of the dragon, out of the mouth of the beast and out of the mouth of the false prophet. They are spirits of demons performing miraculous signs, and they go out to the kings of the whole world, to gather them for the battle on the great day of God Almighty. . . . They gathered the kings together to the place that in Hebrew is called Armageddon" (Revelation 16:13-16).

Here we have the dragon (paganism, Revelation 12:4) the beast (the papacy, Revelation 13:1-3), and the false prophet (apostate Protestantism, Revelation 13:11-15). These are religious avenues through which the spirits of demons are working with miracles to deceive the world. But their day of triumph will end at Armageddon. God is about to rise and slay every giant. There's good news coming. The Bible is full of it. Consider the Old Testament.

Armageddon in the Old Testament

We will look at three Old Testament examples of battles that are precursors to the final great battle of Armageddon.

Canaan versus Israel

Armageddon is first mentioned in Judges 4. Israel languished under cruel oppression for twenty years from Canaan, with its nine hundred iron chariots (verses 1-3). It was a great time of trouble for Israel. They had actually brought it upon themselves. Yet God had not forgotten them. He sent a message through Deborah, a prophetess. "I will lure Sisera, the commander of Jabin's army, with his chariots and his troops to the Kishon River and give him into your hands" (verse 7).

Enter the first wimp recorded in Scripture. Barak, the military commander, replied to Deborah, "If you go with me, I will go" (verse 8). God had just promised him the victory, yet he failed to go out in confidence. It was as if he said, "Deborah, I will go if you hold my hand!" "Then Deborah said to Barak, 'Go! This is the day the Lord has given Sisera into your hands. Has not the Lord gone ahead of you?' " (verse 14). God went ahead of Barak and "routed Sisera and all his chariots and army by the sword" and "all the troops of Sisera fell by the sword; not a man was left" (verses 15, 16). This was a total victory, reminiscent of the Red Sea annihilation of the Egyptian army (Exodus 14).

In fact, just as the Red Sea victory was followed by the song of Moses (Exodus 15), so the victory over the Canaanites was followed by the song of Deborah (Judges 5). Part of that song says, "Kings came, they fought; the kings of Canaan fought at Taanach by the waters of Megiddo" (verse 19), and the place is also called "the river Kishon" (verse 21). Because Kishon is near Megiddo, Armageddon and Kishon refer to the same area. Four things are important, for this battle is a type of the coming Armageddon. God's people were totally outnumbered, the enemy were totally destroyed, God's people were totally delivered, and prophetic ministry was involved.

Baal priests versus Elijah

On Mount Carmel, Elijah was surrounded by 450 prophets of Baal (1 Kings 18:19), and Elijah was a type of the end-time church (Malachi 4:5). Israel wallowed in deep apostasy under King Ahab and Queen Jezebel. The people worshiped Baal; they were Laodicean. They lacked commitment and conviction. Elijah challenged them: "How long will you waver between two opinions? If the Lord is God, follow him; but if Baal is God, follow him" (1 Kings 18:21).

How does this apply to our day? Did it ever occur to you that those who are frightened of final events have an attitude a lot like the attitude of the sinful Israelites back then? The issue is the same: Will we give credence to the power of the enemy, as if Baal is God after all?

We all know the story. The prophets of Baal were all slaughtered in the Kishon Valley, or at Armageddon (verse 40). The story has the same elements as the story of Deborah: there was prophetic involvement; God's people were totally outnumbered; in the end, the enemy were totally destroyed.

Multiple nations versus Judah

A huge army of Moabites, Ammonites, and some Meunites were coming against Jehoshaphat, king of Judah. Alarmed, the king sought the Lord and proclaimed a fast (2 Chronicles 20:1-3). He implored, "O our God, will you not judge them? For we have no power to face this vast army that is attacking us. We do not know what to do." He admitted his utter helplessness, not as a wimp, but as one who would not depend upon self. Helpless, yes, "but our eyes are upon you, " he told God (verse 12). That is the secret. Not looking at the coming crisis, but looking to Christ.

Then God spoke through Jahaziel, "Do not be afraid or discouraged because of this vast army. For the battle is not yours, but God's. . . . You will not have to fight this battle. Take up your positions; stand firm and see the deliverance the Lord will give you. . . . Go out to face them tomorrow, and the Lord will be with you" (verses 15-17). When they began to sing praise to God, He "set ambushes against" the enemies. "They helped to destroy one another." The vast army lay dead on the ground, not even one escaped (verses 22-24). Judah was totally outnumbered, the enemy were totally destroyed, Judah was totally delivered, and the prophet Jahaziel was involved.

So it will be in the future; the whole world will be against God's saints (Revelation 13:11-15), but all the saints' enemies will be destroyed, all the saints delivered, and among them will be the prophetic guidance of dreams and visions (Joel 2:28). The parallels are perfect. We now move from these Old Testament types to the coming battle.

Armageddon in the book of Revelation

Many Christians believe Armageddon is a battle in the Middle East. This viewpoint permeates most denominations. The battle, they claim, concerns Israel. The USSR will invade Israel (not possible now since the breakup of the union), and God will intervene to save Israel. What this view does is to miss the cosmic climax of the great controversy that is just ahead. It is not literal Israel that is involved, but spiritual Israel, God's end-time saints.

Armageddon in Revelation 16

We begin our study with Revelation 16, where the global gathering to Armageddon is mentioned (v. 14). Is it a secular battle about Israel? The context is clear. First, the gathering to the battle involves evil spirits, or spirits of demons. These fallen angels gather people to their side of the battle through miracles (verses 13, 14). That's not the usual way to influence heads of states in negotiations. Nor do generals gather an army that way. This makes it clear that this is not merely a secular battle. But there's more. Look at what is sandwiched between verses 14 and 16: "Behold, I come like a thief! Blessed is he who stays awake and keeps his clothes with him, so that he may not go naked and be shamefully exposed" (verse 15). That's an odd statement if Armageddon is a secular battle. Clearly, this is a message from Christ to His church about His second advent. It is actually a repetition of part of the Laodicean message (Revelation 3:18).

So Armageddon is global, but it pertains to spiritual issues. There are three religious avenues involved, through whom Satan is working, just as Christ works through the three angels' messages (Revelation 14:6-13). There is a double gathering underway. The two sides in the great controversy are preparing for Armageddon.

Armageddon in Revelation 14

Revelation 14 is important for Seventh-day Adventists. The three angels' messages have a prologue and an epilogue. Chronologically, they are arranged as follows: (a) the messages to all the world (verses 6-13), (b) the second-advent part of Armageddon (verses 14-20), and the delivered 144,000 beyond the second advent (verses 1-5). The placement of the future first is to assure us of the outcome. In this way, the structure of chapter 14 functions like the throne scenes that are given before each new section in Revelation—as an assurance that God is still in control.[1]

Armageddon involves the other three angels of Revelation 14. The first three have a message. The last three have a mission. The mission has everything to do with Armageddon. The angels all come from the temple (verses 15, 17, 18). That is, they come from the place of the pre-advent judgment, intent on implementing its verdict. The pre-advent judgment is presented in Daniel 7. Daniel says, "In my vision at night I looked, and there before me was one like a son of man, coming with the clouds of heaven. He approached the Ancient of Days and was led into his presence. He was given authority, glory and sovereign power; all peoples, nations and men of every language worshiped him" (verses 13, 14). Here Christ comes at the end of the judgment process to receive the verdict from the Father, and it indicates that eventually the whole world will worship Christ (compare Revelation 15:4).

So Christ comes on a white cloud to the Father to receive the judgment verdict (Daniel 7:13, 14) and then comes in the second advent on a white cloud to implement the verdict (Revelation 14:14-20). The first angel calls for Christ to take His sickle and reap the harvest of the earth (verses 15, 16). There follows a total deliverance of His saints. The second angel comes out from the temple with a sharp sickle (verse 17). The third angel comes from the altar of the temple and calls for the one with the sharp sickle to reap the earth (verse 18). To whom is he calling, for Christ and the second angel both have sharp sickles? Notice, "the angel swung his sickle on the earth, gathered its grapes and threw them into the great winepress of God's wrath" (verse 19). This reminds us of the "destroying angel" at the Passover,[2] who brought a local death of all the firstborn, typifying the global death of all the wicked.

Armageddon in Revelation 19

Revelation 19 is the fullest account of Armageddon. This time, Christ is pictured riding on a white horse and leading an army on white horses. His eyes are a blazing fire, and He comes with a sharp sword in His mouth, ready to strike the nations. "He treads the winepress of the fury of the wrath of God Almighty" (verses 11-15). "Then I saw the beast [papacy] and the kings of the earth and their armies gathered together to make war against the rider on the horse and his army. But the beast [papacy] was captured, and with him the false prophet [apostate Protestantism] who had performed the miraculous signs on his behalf. . . . The two of them were thrown alive into the fiery lake of burning sulfur. The rest of them were killed with the sword that came out of the mouth of the rider on the horse" (verses 19-21). Here is total destruction of the wicked.

The Battle of Armageddon

The whole world gangs up against God's saints, and the wicked are about to implement the death decree (Revelation 13:15), when Christ manifests His presence with His people.[3] Is it then that the beast and the ten kings will bring the papacy to ruin (Revelation 17:16)? We saw the enemy killing each other in an Old Testament Armageddon (2 Chronicles 20:22-24). God caused this to happen repeatedly in wars (see Judges 7:19-23; 1 Samuel 14:19, 20; Isaiah 19:2; Ezekiel 38:14-23; Haggai 2:22). The angel of death (Revelation 14:19) and Christ (Revelation 19:19-21) will kill those who aren't killed by other people.

Preparation for Armageddon takes place during the sixth plague (Revelation 16:12-16). The battle takes place concurrent with the seventh plague, which I believe is part of the battle. For God has often used hail in battles (Joshua 10:7-14; Job 38:22, 23; Isaiah 30:29, 30). The hailstones used in Armageddon are huge, about a hundred pounds each (Revelation 16:21).

Who are the kings from the East?

Kings from the East are mentioned in the Armageddon passage (Revelation 16:12). Who are they? We know they are not Middle Eastern kings, nor are they from Japan or China in the Far East. In Scripture, if you come from heaven, it is described as "from the east" (Revelation 7:2). In Revelation 4, the Father is seated on the throne, and Christ comes to Him to receive the sealed scroll (verses 1-7). The same throne scene passes into chapter 6. The final verses of chapter 6 portray the second advent. The mighty leaders of the earth are petrified over the second coming and cry out to the mountains and rocks, "Fall on us and hide us from the face of him who sits on the throne and from the wrath of the Lamb! For the great day of their wrath has come, and who can stand?" (Revelation 6:16, 17).

The kings from the East are the Father and the Son, who sweep down together through the heavens to destroy all the wicked who are about to destroy the saints. Jesus spoke of this day. He said to the high priest, during His trial before the

Sanhedrin, "In the future you will see the Son of Man sitting at the right hand of the Mighty One and coming on the clouds of heaven" (Matthew 26:64). Jesus looked beyond those who surrounded Him and were about to put Him to death. He looked to the day when they would grovel in abject terror. Christ will have the last word, and woe to those who are on the other side of the great controversy. Armageddon is coming.

Christ's last word at the cross

In one sense, Christ's death was *the* final event on planet Earth. It was victory day. It meant the destruction of the enemies of Christ and the deliverance of His saints. This was *the* judgment day for all humankind. The double verdict of destruction and deliverance—these are being worked out in the pre-advent judgment verdict and will be implemented in the end-time judgments (see Revelation 16–18) and Armageddon. No wonder Satan hates the cross and does everything to make it of no effect. Because Christ died for us, He provided an eternal refuge for us from Satan and all who follow Him. Nothing can separate us from Christ's love, not even demons and things future (Romans 8:38, 39).

The two second-advent scenes

There is a comparison in Revelation 14 and 19 that is important. In chapter 14, we see Christ riding on a white cloud with a crown on His head. **The scene is peaceful.** He comes to deliver His people. The crown is a *stephanos*, or laurel wreath of victory worn by a winner of an Olympic game. It is the same *stephanos* redeemed humans wear (Revelation 4:4). This chapter pictures Jesus as one of us. He has been through the worst time of trouble, far greater than ours, in Gethsemane and the crucifixion. **In Revelation 14, He comes as the compassionate Son of Man.**

In Revelation 19, He comes on a white horse to make war and judge, to throw the enemy into the fiery lake. He comes with multiple crowns, each one a diadem worn only by royalty. He comes as King of kings. He comes as the conquering God.

What do these two pictures of the second advent say to us

today? They say, "I understand; I know what you will go through. I'll go through it with you" (Hebrews 13:5; Matthew 18:20). "The precious Saviour will send help just when we need it. The way to heaven is consecrated by His footprints."[4] They say also, "I am the King of kings. Do not be afraid of the kings of the world in union with the papacy and apostate Protestantism. They are as a wisp of smoke before Me, the eternal King. Do not be afraid of what they might do against you. I will have the last word. I am coming to destroy them. When languishing in prisons, My "angels will come" to you, "bringing light and peace from heaven."[5]

When John the revelator first saw Christ in vision, Christ's eyes were "like blazing fire" (Revelation 1:14), and a sharp sword protruded from His mouth (verse 16). These point to His coming to rescue us in Armageddon, when the same blazing eyes (Revelation 19:12) and sharp sword (verse 15) will put dread into the enemy. At that day, "you will only observe with your eyes and see the punishment of the wicked. If you make the Most High your dwelling—even the Lord, who is my refuge—then no harm will befall you, no disaster will come near your tent. For he will command his angels concerning you to guard you in all your ways" (Psalm 91:8-11).

Soon we will be thrust into final events. Christ likens them to birth pains (Matthew 24:8). Every mother knows that beyond the pain is the joy of a baby in her arms. Beyond the turbulence ahead is an eternity with our Saviour. Heaven will be cheap enough. Christ will be with us, for "God is our refuge and strength, an ever-present help in trouble" (Psalms 46:1).

---

1. These throne scenes in Revelation are as follows: introduction to seven churches (1:10-20), seven seals (chapter 4–5), seven trumpets (8:2-6), great-controversy chapter (11:19), seven plagues (chapter 15), fall of Babylon (16:18–17:3), second advent (19:1-10), and new earth (21:5-11).
2. Ellen G. White, *Advent Review and Sabbath Herald*, 21 May 1895.
3. *The Great Controversy*, 635, 636.
4. Ibid., 633.
5. Ibid., 627.

ANGELS

Many people are fascinated with angels today. But most people misunderstand who these heavenly messengers are. Pacific Press books can help you and your friends understand the angels who walk with us.

In the Presence of Angels, by E. Lonnie Melashenko and Timothy E. Crosby, will thrill you with modern stories of angel ministry. Readers learn about who angels really are from present-day experiences and from a biblical perspective. This is an excellent gift book.
Paper:US$10.99/Cdn$15.99.

Angels, a compilation of short statements from the pen of Ellen White, is an ideal gift book as well. In the format of popular quotation books, it brings together some of Mrs. White's most poignant comments about angels.
Paper: US$5.99/Cdn$8.99.

The Truth About Angels is a brand new addition to the Christian Home Library. This 320-page reference traces angels' activity from the beginning of time through the time of trouble, and into the earth made new.
Hard cover:US$12.99/Cdn$18.99.

For books about angels, think of your local ABC as the *Angels* Book Center!

Call toll free
1-800-765-6955.

THE END IS NEAR!

End-time events. Adventists love to discuss what's happening now and what's coming next. It's important that we understand our world and what God has planned for it.

If you'd like to know more about this important topic, Pacific Press books can help.

Preparation for the Final Crisis by Fernando Chaij is a classic that continues to sell like a new release. It is popular for use in study groups because of its convenient arrangement of information.

Two recent books by *Signs of the Times* editor Marvin Moore give excellent insights on this topic as well: *Crisis of the End Time*, a book written for Adventist readers, and *The Antichrist and the New World Order*, which is designed for sharing with non-Adventists.

Your Christian Home Library isn't complete if you don't have the recent release *Last Day Events*, which is compiled from the writings of Ellen G. White.

Whether you're looking for personal study aids, something for a study group, or books to share, your local ABC has just what you need!

US$2.99/ Cdn$4.49

US$12.99/ Cdn$18.99

US$10.99/ Cdn$15.99

US$8.99/ Cdn$13.49

Order now from your local ABC, or call toll free 1-800-765-6955.

©1996 Pacific Press Publishing Association 136/81700